About the Author

Derek was Senior Tutor in Accounting at the London Business Schoo[...]
he retired. In 1964 he was appointed as the first lecturer in accounting at the [...]
Manchester Business School. Previously he worked as a management consultant with the P. E. Group. He attended the University of Nottingham, where he obtained an honours degree in Economics and Mathematics. He also studied Organisational Behaviour at the Stanford Business School, as a Foundation for Management Education Fellow. He is a Fellow of the Institute of Chartered Accountants and of the Royal Society of Arts.

Over the years, he has designed and taught on programmes for:

The Bank of America,

Barings International Securities,

British Aerospace,

Canadian Imperial Bank of Commerce,

Courtaulds,

Hambros,

Hilton,

ING,

Paribas,

S. G. Warburg & Co,

3M, and

Unilever.

These programmes took place in Europe, the Far East, Africa, Russia, and South America.

Published by:

In Your Own Words Ltd.

Email: ownwordltd@aol.com

ISBN 978-1-900336-01-7

Copyright Derek Stone © 2014

Web address:

www.understandaccounting.com

Do visit; there is lots of supportive material there

TABLE OF CONTENTS

INTRODUCTION AND ACKNOWLEDGEMENTS

– The need for communication and the role of the language of money.

Communication between managers in different departments is essential. They need a common language so that they can share their aims, evaluate them, and agree a common plan for their businesses. Fortunately the language of money is ready and waiting to be used.

CHAPTER ONE – IT WASN'T ME

- The Separate Business Entity

Andrew wants to start a taxi business and his wife, Joan, suggests that he seeks some help from his financial advisor friend, Richard, in preparing his **business plan**.

CHAPTER TWO – THE NUTS AND BOLTS

- The Transaction Equation

Andrew can hardly believe that the system he is following is **as simple as 1 = 1.**

As they develop his plans, Richard explains things to him, in a simple and chatty way.

CHAPTER THREE – A Question of Time

- Telling the truth, as nearly as we can

It is helpful to **sum up a business's affairs** at the end of each year. This is not as straightforward as one might think, because some transactions have to be estimated.

CHAPTER FOUR – How are we doing?

- The Spreadsheet Overview and the Income Statement Story

Andrew sees that the year can be summed up in different ways: **a trilogy of stories** really, beginning with the income story. He also wants to know how inventories would be handled, and sales taxes too.

CHAPTER FIVE – have we got more money than when we started?

- The Cash Flow Story

Next, and most important of all, where did the money come from, how much of it did the business generate in the year and what did it do with it?

CHAPTER SIX – where are we now?

- The Balance Sheet Story

Finally a photograph of the business in a moment of time – in which it wants to look its best.

CHAPTER SEVEN – Should we get bigger?

- Cost Behaviour And Break–Even Analysis

Andrew looks at costs and revenues from a different point of view. Richard explains fixed and variable costs, break–even charts, and contribution.

CHAPTER EIGHT – What next?

- Modeling The Future

Andrew builds a model of his business on his computer and fleshes out his plans for the next five years. It is a simple model, but that is its utility; **it is easy to build**.

CHAPTER NINE – ARE WE ON COURSE?

- A Matter Of Interpretation

Is the company going to be profitable? Will it be risky? Together with examining its cash flows, some ratios help Andrew discover what is going on inside his business. He feels in control now that he "**Knows his numbers and therefore knows his business.**"

CHAPTER TEN – A LITTLE BIT OF HISTORY – CRACKING THE PACIOLI CODE

-The way that the spreadsheet is really at the heart of traditional accounting systems

In 1494 an Italian monk called **Luca Pacioli** (who was also a respected mathematician) investigated what he called the 'Venetian Method', which was a system for recording commercial transactions. He described the method in an appendix to a textbook, and it has been used in the form that he described it ever since; used by all companies in the world. In this chapter the system is explained and Andycabs' figures are put into this format – known now as '**Double Entry'**. After reading this chapter the terminology will never confuse you again! You will know WHY the system works, as well as HOW; not even all accountants know that!

GLOSSARY

A list of the terms used, with definitions

INTRODUCTION
AND
ACKNOWLEDGEMENTS

'Never ask of money spent
where the spender thinks it went.

Nobody was ever meant
to remember, or invent,
what he did with every cent.'

Robert Frost

Introduction

It seems that this distinguished American poet, was a more than a little out of touch with the world of business; his attitude was likely to result in the sentiments summed up by Richard Armour in this poem:

That money talks,

I'll not deny,

I heard it once,

It said – 'Goodbye'

Not a result that businesses want! They need complete records of 'What they did with every cent' in order to be in control and to comply with legal requirements, including those set by the tax authorities who would otherwise be likely to query their figures; again a situation in which no business wants to find itself.

Communication and the approach taken in this book

As well as being a means of recording a business's activities, the language of money is also a method of communication. The use of specialist terminology *within* departments is *effective*, but it can be a *barrier* to communication *between* them, preventing the managers in different departments from developing common aims and plans for their companies. For this to take place they need a common language and one is there, ready and waiting – the language of money. Most business situations can be expressed in terms of revenues, expenses and cash flows, so once this language is understood, effective communication can take place.

In this book you are going to meet Andrew, who is about to start his own taxi business. This is a relatively simple business, familiar to most of us, but which is both rich in concepts, and simple to understand.

Joan, Andrew's wife, suggests that he should ask his friend, Richard, to help him prepare a business plan. Richard is a financial advisor who helps small and medium sized firms to understand the numbers in their businesses. You will find that Andrew will take nothing for granted, often holding different opinions, and asking lots of questions, which allows Richard to explain the basic concepts in an informal and conversational way. Sometimes they meet at Richard's office and sometimes at their local pub, 'The Foresters'.

Joan is very interested to know how each meeting went, so after each one Andrew summarises what he has learned.

Technical terms are highlighted the first time they are used and their definitions are in the glossary too.

Andrew also gets Richard to explain how inventories and sales taxes are dealt with, even though they are not applicable to a taxi business.

Acknowledgements

I am very grateful to Richard Stone for his many valuable suggestions. Richard is an independent consultant, describing himself as being like a mechanic – analysing where a business has problems and helping it to overcome them. His forte is in building models of a business's activities, which identify ways to improve its operations. More information about his work is on his website- www.themobilefd.com, which is also the origin of my subtitle **"Know Your Numbers, Know Your Business."**

Claude Hitching was joint author with me of the first edition, published in 1984 by Pitmen's. Many of the concepts that we developed together are to be found in this edition too and I am very grateful to him for his inputs.

I am indebted to Scott Ingalls who designed the cover and provided the illustrations that appear on some of the prefaces to the chapters.

My thanks go to Akash also, of iBookservices, who has overseen the conversion of the text into ebook and print on demand form. I am grateful for his patience with my many revisions.

Finally, I want to thank my wife, Denise, whose knowledge of grammar, together with her advice on choice of phrase, has vastly improved the text.

All errors that may remain are, of course, my responsibility.

CHAPTER ONE

THE SEPARATE BUSINESS ENTITY

A business has its own separate identity,
separate, that is, from that of its owners.

All transactions are recorded from the
point of view of the business,
not from the point of view of its owners.

This means a business starts life with nothing.

Money invested in it will create its first asset, cash.

At the same time a liability is created;
it will owe this money to the investors.

It is their capital, and any subsequent profits that
the company creates will also be owed to its owners.

Introduction

"You're home early, Andy, I haven't even started preparing dinner yet. In fact I haven't even chosen a recipe," said Joan, looking up from the cookbook she was thumbing through.

"Well, it's likely to be the last time I'll be early from now on, if you agree with what I am thinking of doing" he replied. "The boss called a meeting today and explained that he has lost two transport contracts, so he is going to have to let three drivers go. He is offering very reasonable redundancy pay and I am thinking of accepting his offer."

Andrew had been with Starlings, a haulage firm, for over ten years. He enjoyed his job, but had often thought about working for himself; this seemed to be his opportunity.

"I went to see Joe on my way home, and he told me that he was thinking of retiring from the taxi business soon. I told him about my situation and he suggested that I should buy his taxi and take over his contract customers, which would be great."

"Wow" his wife replied, "that's a surprise. It's a terrific idea, but can we afford it?"

"Well, I think so. Joe said he wanted £18,000 for the car and that he would introduce me to his contract clients for free. We should be able to raise that amount; there is the redundancy money, we have savings, and we could get a loan from the bank, I expect."

"Then I think you should go ahead, Andy. You have always wanted to be your own boss, and this is a good chance for you to do so."

"It means a lot of hard work you know; I would have to work late into the evenings and at the weekends too" Andrew replied.

"Of course you will, I quite understand that, but will you earn more than you could by continuing to work for someone else?"

"Well, I asked Joe that, and he thinks I should earn much more as the business builds up. He has given me lots of information on costs and fares and I will have to knock these into shape before I go to see the bank manager."

"I could help too, Andy, when the business grows, and when you employ other drivers I will give up my part time bookkeeping job to man the telephone for you, and look after the books. I've got a good idea, why not ask Richard to help you prepare a business plan? You often have a drink with him at our local pub, 'The Foresters', don't you?"

"Employ other drivers? You are even more ambitious than I am! That's a good idea though – to ask Richard for some help – but we have never discussed financial things together; it would be too much like talking shop, him being a financial advisor and all. Still, I'll hint at it tonight over a drink and see how he reacts."

This is where Richard comes into the picture, for, sure enough, after they had finished talking about their local football team's win last Saturday, Andrew raised the topic.

So let's listen in to their conversations, and to Richard's explanations, as they develop plans for Andrew's new business.

The Initial Business Plan

"Look, Richard, I know we haven't talked about financial things before, but something has come up and all of a sudden I need to put a business plan together. Do you think we could break that unwritten rule and talk about it?"

Naturally I agreed to help in any way that I could. He could come round to my office for a chat or maybe we could even talk through some of the issues over a drink at our local pub, so why not start now, for instance?

My immediate response rather took him aback, but there's no time like the present. Looking over his shoulder I could see his car in the car park. It was a real 'I don't care what state it's in provided it can get me from A to B job', if ever there was one.

"Are you planning to get another car?" I asked him.

Andrew saw where I was looking and grinned. "Given the state of this one I reckon I need to. Joe has offered to sell me his, which is just a year old, for the extremely reasonable sum of £18,000, and to introduce me to his contract clients as well."

"Well, that's an excellent start Andrew. What else can you tell me about your plans?"

"Joe has a parking space on the concourse outside our local railway station and I have obtained permission to take over his spot. This should help me get fares from commuters and, as I told you, I also expect to get some regular contract work from businesses in our district. I should get some longer distance work for people who live out in the countryside too.

Joe told me that I should achieve revenues of about £60,000 in the first year. He said that he based this on charging for around 24,000 fare miles at a fare per mile of £2.50. As I will be driving back to base between fares, this will mean that I will be driving about 48,000 miles in all. He gave me lots of other information too. For example, my new car will consume about a litre of fuel every seven miles, so I will need to buy (48,000 /7 =) about 7,000 litres, which, at the current rate of about £1.50 per litre, will cost me about £10,000.

I want to buy a new taximeter, taxi sign, and a fire extinguisher, which together will cost about

£2,000. I shall also have to pay the road tax and insure the car; I estimate those will cost

£2,000 too."

I was impressed.

"OK, so that will get your new car on the road, but have you estimated its running costs, maintenance and so on?"

"Well, I've already mentioned the fuel costs" replied Andrew "and Geoff, who runs my local garage, told me that I ought to allow £8,000 to cover the combined maintenance costs, wear and tear on tyres and the regulation examinations that the authorities require, for the whole of the first year. Then, of course, I should allow for telephone costs. I will use a mobile phone, which will cost me about £2,400 during the first year, I should think."

"And will you do any advertising?" I asked.

"Ah, yes" he said "I'd forgotten about that. I plan to spend about £1,000 on local advertising, business cards, notices in telephone boxes and some advertisements in a few local newspapers."

This was quite a comprehensive list, involving two types of costs some of which will vary according to the number of miles travelled, called **variable costs**, whilst others will not be affected by the number of miles he will drive. These are called **fixed costs**. These distinctions will help Andrew later on to extend his plan to include more years.

Now I had to establish how much money Andrew could invest in this new venture and I wasn't surprised to learn that he had already thought about that too. The money he had received as redundancy pay, combined with some money he and Joan had saved, meant that they would be able to raise £12,000. So it looked as if he would have to approach his bank for some additional funds, since £12,000 wouldn't be enough to pay for the car and its fittings – let alone the insurance, road tax and initial running costs.

"Don't forget I shall need to take money out of the business to cover our living costs too" said Andrew, looking a bit worried.

The Separate Business Entity

Before dealing with all these figures I asked Andrew to think about what he had just said. I wanted him to get away from the idea of 'how *much I could take out of the business'*, and turn the statement round the other way.

"What do you mean?" he asked.

> "Well, you are talking about setting up a new business, so you need to think of it as being totally separate from its owners, you and Joan. It's as if it were another person really. It isn't a case of '*how much can you take out of the business?'*; it's more a question of '*how much the business can afford to pay you in salary each month?*

Another thing we should discuss at this point, Andrew, is whether you and Joan are going to trade as sole traders or are you going to make your business into a **limited liability company**? Once formed it would be a separate legal entity, with whom the owners would have a strictly business relationship. The way a limited liability company keeps its records, and how it presents them to the shareholders, is governed by a series of Companies Acts, but more about them later.

If you operate as sole traders, all of your business's debts will be regarded as your personal debts, even though we choose to think of the business as being a different person. But if it is a limited liability company, then your liability will be limited to the amount of money you put into it in exchange for shares, even if the unthinkable happens, and it fails to succeed. Once you have invested your money in exchange for shares you cannot withdraw it. If you do want your money back, then you will have to sell your shares to someone else."

"Oh, I don't think for a minute that our business will fail, still, it does seem sensible to form it as a limited liability company right from the start."

This means that if Andrew created '*Andrew's Taxis Ltd.'* for instance, it would be a legal and totally separate person from himself, even though his own name might be included as part of its title. This led nicely on to the next question. What had he thought of calling the business, anyway?

"Well, I'm going to call it **Andycabs Ltd**" he said "I can see the name now, painted on the door panel, with my telephone number underneath. Why, Joan thinks that in a few years time, I might be running a fleet of five or six cars, employing other drivers. Or, rather" he added, with a grin "Andycabs might be employing other drivers."

That sounded great and I agreed that from now on we would think of the figures as being relevant to Andycabs, rather than to Andrew and Joan, its owners.

"OK, then all the transactions Andycabs will make will be made in its name, although it will always carry out your orders, because you are the director. In fact you can think of it as being your **robot**, because, if the business is successful, all the extra money it makes it will owe to you and Joan, its shareholders."

Not surprisingly Andrew liked that idea.

"Now, Andrew, we have already agreed that the first thing Andycabs will need before it can start work is a better car than your current one and you told me that Joe will sell it his. That will cost money, so where will it get that from?"

"Well, as you suggested, Joan and I will be investing some of our money in Andycabs Ltd. in exchange for shares and it will have some more from a loan from the bank" he replied.

The first transaction

"So what is the next thing that you will be doing Andrew?"

"Well, I'll be going to see our bank manager to open a new Andycabs Ltd. business account. Then I will write out a cheque for £12,000 from our joint personal account and pay it into its new account, and, while I am there, I am going to ask the bank manager to lend it some money as well, although I shall need a business plan to show him and that's where you come in!"

That was fine. I agreed to come back later to the question of how much of a loan it might need, but, right now, I wanted him to consider the implications of this. He was going to transfer

£12,000 from their joint personal account into Andycabs' new business account. In return he and his wife would own 12,000 one pound shares.

"Right" agreed Andrew, "we will both own 6,000 one pound shares."

So this was going to be the first **financial transaction** to affect the new business. The idea of a transaction is quite straightforward. It literally means a movement across; a *trans – action*, and that is exactly what is happening here. The £12,000 will be moving across from Andrew's and Joan's joint personal account into Andycabs Ltd.'s business account. The shares will be issued at what is known as **nominal value**; their **market value** will differ from this, and it will be decided by how well the company is performing in the future.

Assets and Liabilities

"Now that Andycabs has our £12,000, and we have shares in exchange, how do we describe this transaction in its records?" Andrew asked.

"Well, the £12,000 that Andycabs now has is called an **asset**, and the share capital is called a **liability**. This can be expressed as an equation like this:"

ANDYCABS		
ASSETS	=	LIABILITIES
CASH	=	SHARE CAPITAL
12,000	=	12,000

"Hmm" commented Andrew "I think you need to explain how the words *asset* and *liability* are used in business a bit more. I don't want to get it wrong as this seems essential to me"

"Well, as you can see from the equation above, the business starts off with one asset, cash. In a way it is a strange asset as it is unlike all the other operating assets that Andycabs will have."

"What do you mean, exactly?" Andrew asked.

"Well, in order to earn operating profits cash has to be converted into operating assets. Then, at the very end of their lives, these will be converted back into cash and, if it has been successful, it will have more cash than it started with; this extra will be owed to its owners, of course. Cash is an asset, but it is more a facilitating one rather than an operating one."

"So what is an operating asset then?"

"An operating asset is something that will add value and eventually cash, to the business. It could be a short term asset, like inventory, or it could be something which will last for a long time and which will create cash as it is used over its lifetime, like Andycabs' car."

"What exactly is a liability then?"

"Well, a liability, on the other hand, is an obligation to pay cash to someone at some time in the future."

"So why did you tell me that Share Capital is a liability? You told me earlier that once we had invested our money in Andycabs Ltd, by buying shares in it, we could not take it out again. You said that if we wanted to get our money out we would have to sell our shares to others."

"Remember that we are looking at things from Andycabs Ltd.'s point of view, not yours. From its point of view share capital is a liability; it owes it to its owners. As I told you earlier you should think of Andycabs Ltd as being a person, a robot if you like, but definitely a legal entity separate from its owners. If things go badly and it closes down, then it will owe whatever is left to its shareholders in proportion to the number of shares each of them hold. By the way, Andrew, let's drop the 'Ltd' phrase from now on, we know it's going to be one"

"Good idea; but close down, what a terrible thought" said Andrew "but I do understand what you mean."

Andrew pointed at the equation I had written. "When the business makes a profit – not *if*, Andrew was always the optimist – how will you record that? Say that, at the end of the first year, its cash has increased from £12,000 to £18,000, that would be a profit, wouldn't it? So, would its cash go up by £6,000 and the share capital goes up to balance it, like this":

ANDYCABS		
ASSETS	=	LIABILITIES
CASH	=	SHARE CAPITAL
12,000	=	12,000
6,000	=	6,000

It was a decent attempt but I had to tell him that the *Share Capital* heading could only be used when shares were issued.

"So how would this profit be recorded then? You said Andycabs was our robot and would owe it to us, therefore, it must be its liability surely?"

He was right again. "The way round it is easy; if we cannot use the headings that we have, then we just introduce another one. I call it my operating rule *'if in doubt, open a new column'* and we will need a new heading to record the profit under, so what shall we call it?"

"Um, profit, I should think, because that is what it is."

"I agree with you Andrew, but nowadays it's often called **Income,** so let's use that as our new column heading. Any profits that Andycabs makes will increase its income."

So we have:

ANDYCABS				
ASSETS	=	LIABILITIES		
CASH	=	SHARE CAPITAL	+	INCOME
12,000	=	12,000		
6,000	=			6,000

"I see," said Andrew, after studying this carefully. "It seems a bit odd at first, I mean, seeing income as a liability, but on reflection it does make sense, since poor old Andycabs owes the results of all its hard work to its shareholders so, from its point of view, it is a liability"

Andycabs' business life, like every other business life, will involve it in a series of financial transactions, so it's not possible to jump to the income figure straight away, as I just did in order to explain the principle, but we will get there in the end.

The Andycabs taxi business has been born – if only on paper – and we have recorded its first transaction.

"This is extremely interesting Richard, but it's getting a bit late though, and I think I had better make a move homewards. Do you think we could meet tomorrow to continue?"

"Of course Andrew, I'm free in the afternoon; let's meet here for lunch and we can continue then."

When Andrew got home Joan was eager to hear how things went. "It was fantastic; Richard was more than ready to help me, and we are meeting tomorrow, as its Saturday, for lunch at the pub."

"Do tell me all about it, Andy; I'm very interested in what you have learned today." "OK, Joan, I'll summarise it for you.

Summary

Business entity

"The first thing Richard explained to me was that every business should be regarded as a totally separate entity from its owners, as if it were a person in its own right. Initially, it will have no funds until its owners invest some money in it. This money will be the owners' capital and, in our case, we can invest £12,000 in the business.

So, looking at this investment from Andycabs' point of view, it receives £12,000 in cash, which is its asset, and it is balanced by a liability of equivalent value – i.e., our investment – its share capital. Strictly speaking, this £12,000 is not actually hard cash because it is in Andycabs' bank account; so whenever I talk about its 'cash', remember that this is shorthand for 'cash and bank account' amounts.

Transaction

We recorded Andycabs' first financial transaction, the movement of £12,000 from our personal account to Andycabs' new business account, in return for 12,000 one pound shares. Andycabs now has an asset of £12,000, balanced by a liability of £12,000, the share capital. Because all businesses record both sides of every transaction, the total value of their assets always equals the total value of their liabilities.

Richard used a simple equation to illustrate the point 'Assets = Liabilities' and he is going to explain more about this to me tomorrow."

"That's great, Andrew, I am glad you plucked up your courage and asked him for help. Please keep me updated with a summary like this after all your meetings."

And Andrew promised that he would.

CHAPTER TWO

THE TRANSACTION EQUATION

The transaction equation is a simple device for recording
the monetary aspect of any business decision.

Accounts receivable, accounts payable,
prepayments, and accruals
are discussed,
as is the way that they affect cash flow.

Introduction

When Andrew arrived at 'The Foresters', he was still musing over the picture I had put into his mind about a business being like a robot, working tirelessly for the benefit of its lord and master. The idea appealed to him.

This may sound a bit tough on the business, but the idea has a great deal going for it. It means that everything the company has in its possession it obtained from money it owes to someone else, so the total value of its assets must always equal the total value of its liabilities; a convenient rule that makes it easy to record all the transactions that Andrew is planning will take place.

Setting up the business

At our last meeting we recorded the first transaction equation that would affect Andrew's new taxi business. This equation recorded the transfer of £12,000 of Andrew and Joan's money into the new Andycabs business account, but that would not be enough to get the business on its feet, or 'on the road', as Andrew put it. The car he is going to buy from Joe is going to cost

£18,000. In addition, the first year's tax and insurance costs, will amount to £2,000 and the car fittings, and other initial costs, come to another £2,000. Then there is £1,000 for business cards and some local advertising. Andycabs will have used up quite a bit of money even before it buys the fuel that will be needed to get the car moving, so it will need some additional funds from somewhere. Fortunately Andrew had already mentioned his bank manager, with whom he had an excellent credit record, as the most obvious person to talk to, and hopefully the bank would make Andycabs a loan. Andrew felt that it would need to borrow £10,000, repayable perhaps over two years. This would attract interest charges, which would probably cost Andycabs £700 in its first year.

"My goodness, that's a lot of estimates, how are we going to record them so that I don't get into a muddle?" Andrew asked.

"That's where the 'assets = liabilities' idea comes in" I replied, "we can use it to record all these transactions. I call it a transaction spreadsheet and we are going to use it to create your business plan, starting with the very first transaction."

The Transaction Spreadsheet

Figure 2.0 – Andycabs' first transaction

						Cash	=	Share Cap.						
1	Capital invested					12,000	=	12,000						

"That's neat," said Andrew "let's set it up on my new computer."

"A good idea, Andrew, and it will make life easier for us when we want to introduce new headings too. Now, let's just think about the £10,000 loan for the moment. How should we record that in the transaction equation?"

Andrew had no trouble at all with the first half of this equation. He could see that Andycabs' cash will be increased by £10,000, and he entered that in the cash column. That was fine, but he hesitated when I asked him where he would enter the other side of the equation.

"Well, I can't add it to the share capital column, because it's not an issue of new shares. I'll follow your tip and head up a new column. **Bank Loan**, I'll call it."

"Fine, if in doubt, open a new column" I agreed.

There is no limit to the number of columns that could be used, although it will be easier to follow what's going on if all of Andycabs' transactions can be fitted onto one page. Remember the rule, however, if you can't see a column that fits the transaction you want to record, just open another one. It's as easy as that.

Figure 2.1 – Entering the bank loan

						Cash	=	Share Cap.		Bank Loan				
1	Capital invested					12,000	=	12,000						
2	**Bank loan**					**10,000**	=			**10,000**				
							=							

Now Andycabs has a total of (£12,000 + £10,000 =) £22,000 cash; £12,000 of this came from share capital, and the other £10,000 from a bank loan. We can see how much money there is, and also see where it came from.

"Right" agreed Andrew, "so now it will have sufficient cash for it to go out and buy a car and pay for the road tax, insurance, and all those other things. Let's start with the car."

Andrew figured that the car had to be an asset, so he headed up another asset column called Car. He entered £18,000 in that, but then had to think a bit about the other part of the equation. "Let's see, none of the liabilities will be affected by this purchase, will they?"

"No, they won't. But what will Andycabs use to pay for the car?"

The answer was emphatic. "Cash, oh, I see, I will have to reduce the cash column." So Andrew entered – £18,000 in the cash column.

Figure 2.2 – Buying the car

						Cash	=	Share Cap.		Bank Loan				
1	Capital invested					12,000	=	12,000						
2	Bank loan					10,000	=			10,000				
3	**Car purchase**	**18,000**				**−18,000**	=							
							=							

"But wait a minute" he said "that looks different to the first two transactions; there is nothing on the other side of the equation is there?"

There isn't, but the equation is still valid, because £18,000 – £18,000 = 0; Andycabs has used up part of its facilitating asset, cash, and replaced it with an operating one.

The assets now consist of a car that cost £18,000, which reduced the cash to £4,000 but the total assets still add up to £22,000. The liabilities are made up of £12,000 in share capital plus the bank loan of £10,000, so both sides add up to £22,000, as so they should.

We moved on to the purchase of the car fittings, the taxi sign, fare meter, fire extinguisher, and other initial costs, all of which will total £2,000. In reality, these should have their own columns, but I suggested to Andrew that he should include them in the car column in order to save space. I asked him to total the columns (Line 5), so that he could see how far Andycabs had got.

"Wow, it balances! What shall I call this subtotal?"

"Well, you are ready to start trading now, so this is a snapshot of the business at that moment in time; it's called its opening balance sheet. It's also known as a **trial balance**, because if it doesn't balance then something must be wrong."

"Does that mean that if it does balance all is ok?"

"No. Things might have been left out, put in the wrong columns, even have had the wrong figures put in. That's why it has to be checked to the original transactions by someone. In big business they will be the **auditors**."

"Auditors, Joan has told me about them. Not her favourite people, they always seem to find some mistakes. Anyway, I'll add the fittings now"

Figure 2.3 – Adding the fittings

							Cash	=	Share Cap.		Bank Loan				
1	Capital invested						12,000	=	12,000						
2	Bank loan						10,000	=			10,000				
3	Car purchase	18,000					−18,000	=							
4	**Car fittings**	**2,000**					**−2,000**	=							
5	Balance Sheet year 0	20,000					2,000	=	12,000		10,000				

Each of these three transactions has been recorded in two places; one shows where the money went and the other shows where it came from.

Then Andrew asked me "About these columns – when you introduce a new one, how do you know what order to put them in?"

"Well, I like to put the most long lived assets in the furthest column on the left and the same for the liabilities too. As you will see later this fits in with how financial statements are presented in the UK."

Andrew then said, "Hold on a minute, you just said '*in the UK*'. Does that mean that other countries do this differently?"

"Yes it does. In America, as in many European countries, the shortest lived items come first, and the longest lived ones are shown after them."

"Ah, well" said Andrew, philosophically "I'm not surprised; both Americans and Europeans drive on the opposite side of the road to us, as well!"

Revenues and expenses

Andycabs' new car will be standing in the garage, resplendent with meter, fire extinguisher, and taxi sign. It will have cost £20,000 in all, and Andycabs will still have £2,000 in the bank.

"So, Andrew, how do you think the road tax, insurance and licence fees, costing in total

£2,000, should be entered? Should they be added to the car column?"

"No, I don't think you can do that. Andycabs only buys the car once, but these are items that it will have to pay for every year."

"Yes. So, what effect will these costs have on the business?"

Andrew thought about this, and concluded that they would reduce its profits in the income statement, which is exactly what I wanted him to say. They are called **expenses**, and, as he had said, expenses reduce profits, whilst **revenues**, increase them.

This led nicely to the following definition of profit:

Profit = Revenues – Expenses

Andrew had quite rightly pointed out earlier that any profit that Andycabs made would be owed to its shareholders; its liability to them would be increased by that amount and it would be recorded in the income column. That's why we placed the income column on the liabilities side of the spreadsheet. From our point of view the terms 'profit' and 'income' are interchangeable terms. Thus, the Assets = Liabilities formula became

$$Assets = Liabilities + Income$$

Since profits are recorded in the income column, we can expand the formula above by replacing *Income* with '*Revenues – Expenses*' like this:

$$Assets = Liabilities + Revenues - Expenses$$

If we add expenses to both sides we get:

$$Assets + Expenses = Liabilities + Revenues - Expenses + Expenses$$

The '+ *Expenses – Expenses*' elements on the right hand side cancel each other out, leaving us with:

$$Assets + Expenses = Liabilities + Revenues$$

"Add expenses to both sides," said Andrew, "my goodness that gets rid of a mental block I've had since school days. I was taught '*take it to the other side and change the sign*', and I never did understand why."

Then he added "I say, that's a bit funny isn't it, having expenses on the same side as assets? Assets are nice things to have, whereas expenses Andycabs could do without!"

But in a fundamental way they are the same. You can think of an operating asset as '*an expense waiting to happen*'. Take Andycabs' car, for example. It is an asset of the business, but, over time, it will get '*used up*' and turned into an expense through something called **depreciation**. This is such an essential item that it needs further discussion, so it will be revisited later on.

Some assets are extremely short lived, a telephone call, for instance. This adds value to the business and so it is an operating asset – assuming it's a business call – but it is used up immediately and so it becomes an expense. Such expenses have been described as being '*assets that were 100% depreciated in the trading period*' – not a bad way of looking at it.

I asked Andrew what he considered the most significant element in any company's expenditure, apart from the money it spends on things like inventories and longer lived assets, and he replied, without any hesitation at all, that it had to be the employees' wages. I then asked if he would regard the people who earned the wages as assets of the business. He saw the drift, and agreed that the employees were probably the most valuable assets that any company could have.

"Right, I said "but the company doesn't own its employees, does it? The wages it pays them are for the use of the particular expertise or abilities that they provide. The company receives a positive benefit from using up these services during the period for which the wages are paid. When an asset has been used up, it has been expensed, so wages are an expense to the business."

Andrew smiled. "Hmm I see" he said "that makes sense to me, but how do I apply it when entering Andycabs' fuel, for example? When it is first bought it is in the tank, not used up, so should I regard it as an asset, inventory, when I enter it on the spreadsheet?"

"It is, when it is actually in the tank" I agreed "but it will be fully expensed, or used up, during the period in which it is purchased. There is no point in adding it into an inventory column, and then taking almost all of it out again. There will probably be some left in the tank at the end of the year, but not enough to be bothered about. Most of what was bought will be used up in the year, so you may as well charge Andycabs' fuel purchases to the income column as expenses straight away."

"OK, I'm getting warmer" Andrew assured me. "I suppose the same would be true for things like telephone calls, postage, and all those other things that are expensed in business."

"That's right, Andrew. You've got it."

He still wasn't quite convinced. "Well, what about road tax, insurance and licence fees? They must presumably be expenses, too, although it won't use those up within a couple of days of paying for them."

"No, that's true I agreed, "Andycabs will be paying for these in advance, probably for the whole of the next year. However, you have to remember that we are now talking about all the things that are going to happen to Andycabs within its first year of operations. It will have used up the first payment for these things by the end of it, which means that they too, can be entered straight into the income column as negative figures. The second payment that it has to make in the first year will be a **prepayment**, and we can consider how to enter that when we come to it"

"I see, so we're back to this question of time again, aren't we? If you buy something, to use within the year, it's an expense, but if you buy something that you intend to keep and use for more than a year, it's an asset. Is it really as straightforward as that?"

"Yes, it really is" I assured him.

Strictly speaking there should be a separate column for every item of revenue and expense, as well as for every type of asset and liability. Most businesses make many sales of their services or products every day, and buy them daily too, so they use two subsidiary records; one to record all daily sales and one to record daily purchases. These are called sales and purchases day books. At intervals, maybe daily, weekly or monthly, these would be added up and their totals entered into the main financial records. That's the way to stay in control; keeping an eye on everything that is going on. But a very large spreadsheet would be needed to mirror that – so, to keep things simple, let's use just one column to record both revenue and expense items – the income column. In practice all of this information is computerised of course.

"By the way, do you remember that I mentioned the Companies Acts a little while ago? Well, one requirement of the Acts is that expenditures made on items which will last for more than one year have to be differentiated from those that will be charged directly to the year's income statement. The former are called **capital expenditures**, like buying the car, and the others are called **revenue expenditures** because they will be 'used up' within the year in which they were incurred."

"That seems to be a funny term to me – revenue and expenditure being used in the same breath," said Andrew. I sympathised with him, but that's what they are called in order to identify the expenses that will be charged against revenues in the trading year. It does confuse the situation, because financial people also include as expenses items that have been 'used up' in the year even though they have not been paid for by the end of Andycabs' financial year. They even include as expenses items that have only been estimated at that time too. We just have to live with this use of the word.

"That's a pity, but I think I understand it" said Andrew "but let's get back to this year's road tax etc. I would like to enter them now, in total they come to £2,000, don't they?"

"Yes, and while you are at it why don't you enter the advertising cost of £1,000 too? But, first of all, where are you going to put this income column, Andrew? Will it go with Andycabs' assets, or its liabilities?"

"Oh, that's easy" he replied, "we've already discussed that. If Andycabs makes a profit, it will automatically owe that to its owners, us. After all it is our robot. That makes it a liability, but shall I position its column to the right of the share capital column or the bank loan one?"

"You are right that it does belong to the shareholders and it would be correct to put it next to their column, but I like to position it as the final column in the spreadsheet because it is going to sum up lots of entries as we progress. We can transfer its final balance to a column next to the share capital column when we have finished."

"OK then, I'll do that." And Andrew soon had the numbers entered.

Figure 2.4 – Recording the tax, insurance and advertising

		Car			Cash	=	Share Cap.	Bank Loan				Income
5	Balance Sheet year 0	20,000			2,000	=	12,000	10,000				
6	Tax, insurance, etc.				−2,000	=						−2,000
7	Advertising				−1,000	=						−1,000

Despite the fact that this was right, he seemed to be rather concerned about something. "What's the problem, Andrew?"

"Well, I have just noticed how quickly Andycabs seems to be getting through its cash. By the time it has bought the car and its fittings, and paid for the road tax, insurance, and licence fees, it hasn't any money left at all. Perhaps I should ask the bank manager to lend it more than

£10,000?

Maybe, but I doubted whether it would be necessary.

This problem always arises when summarising a year's transactions on a spreadsheet, because it looks as if all the items occur just once in the year and in the sequence shown. This is not true, of course. Andycabs will be receiving regular revenues from customers and paying out regular amounts too. So any subtotals of its partly filled in spreadsheet will not indicate the actual situation that will be occurring week by week. Weekly spreadsheets would capture that but, at this stage, that would distract from the explanation of the basic structure of the system.

"I'll say it would" said Andrew fervently "let's stick to just this one annual spreadsheet, I get the message."

We have recorded the start–up expenses; everything from now on will be part of the ongoing operational costs of the business. Most of these expenses will not be incurred until there are also some revenues involved, so if any unforeseen short–term shortages should arise, these can be taken care of by arranging a small overdraft facility at the time. It is also to Andycabs' advantage to keep the size of the loan down to a minimum, because it will be charged interest on its outstanding balance.

"That settles it, then" agreed Andrew. I had thought it would.

Next, to Andrew's pleasure, I wanted to consider the revenue Andycabs would earn. Andrew had already told me that he was expecting this to be about £60,000. It was not likely that this would all come in as cash immediately, though, because Andycabs would have several contract customers, some that Joe would introduce and probably others, as there was quite a lot of light industry in the neighbourhood.

Andrew nodded. He was sure that this would be the case, but couldn't quite see what difference it made.

The point is that these firms will expect to settle their bills on a monthly basis, in the same way that Andycabs will want to settle its fuel and maintenance bills with the local garage. This means that some of the work done by Andycabs would be undertaken on **credit**, and these credit customers would pay their bills some time after the services have been rendered.

Accounts Receivable and Accounts Payable

"So, Andrew, how much of the £60,000 will be cash fares, and how much will be on account?" After a few moments thought Andrew reckoned that the split in the first year would probably be about 80% in cash (£48,000), and the rest (£12,000), on credit.

He had no doubt at all about how he would record its cash receipts in the transaction spreadsheet, but how should he record the amounts owed by contract customers?

He was ready for that one. A broad grin spread over his face as he pointed to the spreadsheet. "Head up another column" he said, but his grin faded when I asked him what he would call it.

"Ah. Now, let me see" he said, rubbing his chin "if Andycabs provides a service to someone, and allows them time before paying for these services, then it will have to wait to receive those payments, so how about 'Accounts Receivable'?"

He'd got it in one. **Accounts Receivable** is the term used to describe customers who owe money for goods or services received, but for which they have not yet paid. They are also known as **Debtors**.

Conversely, **Accounts Payable** refers to suppliers to whom money is owed for goods or services that they have provided.

Accounts receivable and accounts payable (also called **Creditors**) are both part of the same facilitating asset type as cash; only time separates them. Time is, however, of considerable significance here as it affects the rate at which cash moves into or out of the business. **Cash is the lifeblood** of the business, so any significant interruption to the inflows can be serious. If the inflows slowdown, one response might be to slowdown the outflows too, that is, not pay the accounts payable on time either, but that could cause Andycabs to have problems with its suppliers. *Andrew should keep an eye on its accounts receivable and payable at all times.*

"I see," said Andrew, "so its credit customers will be classed as its accounts receivable between the time they use Andycabs' services and the time they settle their accounts. Is that right?"

"Yes it is, Andrew, and since Andycabs earns revenue when it provides a service, whether it is paid for at the time or not, all the revenue that it earns in the year has to be entered in the income column, even if some of it has not yet been paid for or even invoiced."

"Hmm, right, I understand that now and I am ready to make those entries. The £48,000 cash transaction is easy, it will increase Andycabs' cash and it will also increase its profit, so it is simply a matter of writing it in the cash column, and balancing it in the income column."

I waited to see how Andrew would tackle the credit fares. He headed up one of the asset columns, placing it between the car and the cash columns, and when I asked him why he had done this, he replied "Well, it's because they owe Andycabs money, isn't it? In other words, I am providing a taxi service for cash that hasn't arrived yet. It will arrive eventually though, and when it does, it will be an asset. So I figured that accounts receivable must be a sort of delayed cash asset. I placed it between the car and cash columns because it is less durable than the car but not as liquid as cash."

Figure 2.5 – Entering the revenue items

		Car	A/Cs Rec	Cash	=	Share Cap.	Bank Loan			Income
5	Balance Sheet year 0	20,000		2,000	=	12,000	10,000			
6	Tax, insurance, etc.			–2,000	=					–2,000
7	Advertising			–1,000	=					–1,000
8	**Revenue – cash**			**48,000**	=					**48,000**
9	**Revenue – credit**		**12,000**		=					**12,000**

"Terrific, Andrew, I couldn't have put it better myself."

Now let's move on to the next items of expense – namely, the cost of fuel, £10,000, and the costs of the regulation inspections, maintenance and tyres, £8,000. They fit in nicely here, because as I had just pointed out, these are also likely to be credit transactions. Andrew has known Geoff Marsden, the owner of The Fourways Garage, for many years, and has always gone to him for his own fuel. It seems perfectly safe to assume that Geoff would be prepared to open a credit account for the supply of fuel and maintenance services to Andycabs.

The only other outstanding items on Andrew's list were his anticipated telephone costs of £2,400, and the interest relating to the bank loan (£700). "So, Andrew, since you will be using a 'pay as you go' phone, why not enter both of these items as cash items and then extract another trial balance, to make sure that the total value of Andycabs' assets is still equal to the total value of its liabilities?"

Figure 2.6 – Entering the fuel, maintenance etc. expenses, and interest items

		Car	A/Cs Rec	Cash	=	Share Cap.	Bank Loan	A/Cs Pay		Income
5	Balance Sheet year 0	20,000		2,000	=	12,000	10,000			
6	Tax, insurance, etc.			–2,000	=					–2,000
7	Advertising			–1,000	=					–1,000
8	Revenue – cash			48,000	=					48,000
9	Revenue – credit		12,000		=					12,000
10	**Fuel costs**				=			10,000		–10,000
11	**Maintenance/Tyres**				=			8,000		–8,000
12	**Telephone**			–2,400	=					–2,400
13	**Loan interest**			–700	=					–700
14	**Trial balance**	**20,000**	**12,000**	**43,900**	=	**12,000**	**10,000**	**18,000**		**35,900**

It didn't take him long to make these entries, including explaining to me that he had put his new *accounts payable* column between the bank loan column and the income column because it was more liquid than the bank loan. He added the columns up, and he was very pleased when his trial balance did indeed balance with a total of £75,900 on each side.

"Gee, that's enough for this session, I need to go away and think about it, and summarise it for Joan – if I can remember it all."

Summary

Joan had not arrived back from work when Andrew got home. He decided to surprise her by getting some dinner together, but, after looking in the fridge, he admitted defeat; it looked just too difficult. So, when Joan came in he said, "I've lots to tell you but let's try that new Italian pizza place and we can talk over dinner." "Great, I'm starving and apparently their 'four season's' pizza is really good."

After their orders had arrived, Joan said "Come on Andy, tell me about your day."

The Transaction equation

"Well, Richard started by telling me that every business transaction could be expressed in the transaction equation

$$\text{'Assets = Liabilities'},$$

that would show precisely where the subject of each transaction came from, and where it went to.

He then expanded this to record profits, (he said its modern term is income) like this:

$$\text{Assets = Liabilities + Income}$$

Income is on the right hand side of the equation because any profits Andycabs creates it owes to its shareholders.

Then, since 'Income = Revenues – Expenses' he wrote:

$$\text{Assets = Liabilities + Revenues – Expenses}$$

And then he got rid of the minus sign by adding expenses to both sides, like this: Assets + Expenses = Liabilities + Revenues – Expenses + Expenses

The '+ *Expenses – Expenses*' elements on the right hand side cancel each other out, leaving us with:

$$\text{Assets + Expenses = Liabilities + Revenues}$$

"That looks a bit weird," said Joan "having assets and expenses on the same side, as if they were the same."

"That's just what I said," exclaimed Andrew. "I'll get to Richard's explanation in a minute when I've told you about the revenues and expenses part of the discussion.

Income

In order to save space, we only using one column to record all the entries that affect Andycabs' income. We put it on the liabilities side of the spreadsheet, because any profit made by Andycabs will automatically increase its liability to its shareholders (us). We entered revenues as plus figures, and expenses as minuses, since they respectively increased or decreased the income column.

Revenues and Expenses

Revenue is earned when a service has been rendered, even if not paid for by the year end, and even if the invoice has not yet been sent to the contract passenger. Richard told me that all revenues have to be included in the income column, including estimated ones, and have to be balanced by entering the same amount in the accounts receivable column. This timing difference means that the revenue figure for the year will not be the same as the cash figure that will be received from customers in that year.

Expenses represent the using up of assets, and he defined an asset as anything that is intended to create cash for the company, whether it is a long–lived asset or an extremely short–lived one such as a telephone call, or fuel for the car. He said that cash itself is a facilitating asset that needs to be converted into operating assets. These create cash over their lifetimes, and, at the end of their lives, create even more cash when they are sold, unless they are scrapped, of course. Expenses are not the same as **expenditures**. Expenditures take place when cash is paid, which may be in a different period to the one in which the expense is charged to the income column. Unfortunately the word 'expenditure' is also used in a slightly different way that is not necessarily related to the movement of cash; it is used to differentiate the *types* of expenditures that are made, so **capital expenditures** relate to long-lived assets whilst **revenue expenditures** relate to those expenses that will be charged to the income column in the year.

All these things represent money paid for the use of a service, for example, that given by the employees, or the telephone company. He told me that it is often said that the employees represent the biggest asset that a company can have, but that this particular asset was not actually the people; it was the service and expertise that they provided. It becomes a '*used up*' asset – a **revenue expense** – during the year and is charged to the income column.

It occurred to me that the purchase of an airline ticket would be another example. It represents the right to travel on the service provided by the operator, and, whilst the ticket is an asset when it is purchased, it only stays that way until the journey starts. From that point on it is being consumed, or expensed."

"You did cover a lot of ground this afternoon Andy, let's order coffee before you go on. What topic came next?"

"Richard went on to explain all about accounts receivable and payable. He told me that an accounts receivable passenger is someone who has been supplied with goods or services, but who has not yet paid for them. Conversely, an accounts payable supplier is a credit supplier from whom Andycabs has received goods or services for which it has not yet paid. He said that accounts receivable and accounts payable have the effect of interrupting the flow of cash into or out of a company. Accounts receivable are assets, since they represent cash that is due, but has not yet arrived, while accounts payable are liabilities, because they represent an amount that has still to be paid. Both are extensions of cash and closely related to it so they are facilitating things too. The terms 'accounts receivable' and 'accounts payable' are sometimes called debtors and creditors respectively. He emphasised that cash is the lifeblood of the business and that I must keep an eye on the inflows and outflows extremely carefully. Then he went on to explain trial balances to me."

"Trial balances, I know all about them," said Joan, whose part time job was as a bookkeeper to a local business. "But what did he tell you about them?"

Trial Balance

"He told me that the term **trial balance** refers to a subtotal of all the columns in our spreadsheet and that it lists all the balances in a company's records. This is to check whether the total of all the asset and expense balances is equal to the total of all the liabilities and revenue ones. He explained that even if it did balance this would not ensure that every entry had been made correctly, because there may have been some compensating errors lurking around that still have to be traced. However, a balancing trial balance is a reasonable start, he said. I found it all very interesting but I was glad when that session ended. I am meeting him in his office tomorrow evening after I finish work. By the way, I am going to tell my boss that I will be accepting his offer to leave the firm with the redundancy pay packet he had described, if you still agree, of course"

"Yes, I certainly do. Well, I did enjoy eating out for a change. Let's get the bill now though, Andy, and make our way home."

CHAPTER THREE

A QUESTION OF TIME

'Here today and gone tomorrow'.

We have seen that for some assets, this is not true.

They will be used by the business for years;
not only used, but 'used up' too,
and this has to be recognised.

This will be achieved through depreciation,
a topic that alarmed Andrew somewhat.

The aim is to produce a 'true and fair view' of Andycabs'
business at the end of its trading year.

A True and Fair View

Monday had been a busy day for me and I was just enjoying a refreshing cup of tea when Andrew arrived. Needless to say he had a cup too, and then we crossed over to my conference table and got down to work.

After uploading the spreadsheet, Andrew pointed to the trial balance and asked me "Have we nearly finished developing my plan then? Because I have entered all the estimates I made – apart from my salary, of course."

"Well, not quite yet, there are still some more things to put in. Remember that I mentioned earlier that depreciation was a topic of such importance that we should examine it in more detail? Well, that time has now arrived. First, however, let's think again about the £20,000 that will be spent on purchasing the car and its fittings. The car is going to enable Andycabs to earn revenues for several years, so you can also think of that amount as being a prepayment for those future revenues. So it is only fair to match the purchase cost of the car over the years that you will be using it, with those revenues. In a way Andycabs is *using up* the car as it uses it year by year. So Andrew, at the moment the car and its fittings are in the trial balance at their initial cost. Do you think they should be included at that figure in Andycabs' financial statements at the end of its first year?"

"Well, no, I suppose not after what you have just told me. Andycabs will have been using the car for a year by then, won't it? That wouldn't be fair."

He couldn't have put it better. The fact that Andycabs has *'used up'* some of the car, and its fittings, during the year has to be expressed as an expense incurred in that year. Andycabs' income column will benefit from all the revenues earned, and it should be charged with all of the expenses incurred in the year, whether or not the related payments were actually received or made during that time. This has to include a charge for the *'using up'* of its long-lived assets during the year, in Andycabs' case, its car and fittings.

All companies have to ensure that their financial statements reflect a **true and fair view** of their financial situation at the end of the trading period to which they relate, in Andycabs' case, its first year, and this has to include a charge to match part of the cost of its long term assets with the revenue generated from using them. This is known as the **'matching principle'**.

Depreciation

Andrew agreed that this was reasonable. "The question is Andrew, how shall we achieve this? Would you charge the whole cost of Andycabs' car and fittings against income in its first year?"

"What, the whole of that £20,000! I mean, we have agreed that the car will be something that it will use for several years. It wouldn't be fair to charge the whole of its initial purchase price against the first year's revenue, surely? Remember what you just told me about matching the cost of the car over its life with the revenues it creates for Andycabs each year."

"So what will you do then?"

"Well, I will work out the number of years that Andycabs expects to use the car, and spread its cost evenly over that period."

"OK, but you might want to sell it before it reaches the end of its life, when it gets a bit tired looking, for example."

"Well, in that case, I will deduct the amount I expect to get for it before I work out the annual charge. In that way, each year will receive its fair charge for the use of the asset and this fits in with your matching principle too"

"Yes, and that's what we call **depreciation**" I explained "it is the charge made against a company's trading revenues for the using–up of its **noncurrent assets**, such as Andycabs' car. It is not a cash transaction, because that took place at the time of the original purchase, but it is certainly a charge that has to be made against income. It isn't only just a question of fairness

– Company Law requires that all assets with limited useful lives must be depreciated. The one type of asset that is not depreciated is land, because its useful working life is virtually unlimited

– unless you are mining it, but that is a particular case, which is not relevant to Andycabs."

So now Andrew had to estimate the car's useful life, and whether Andycabs would get any money for it when it disposed of it. He didn't like the idea of being tied down to exact figures over something as uncertain as this, but he realised that he had to have a go. After some deliberation, he suggested that we should use a five–year life and allow for Andycabs selling it for £5,000 after five years.

"That will give us a nice round figure of (£20,000 – £5,000) divided by 5 = £3,000 a year" he said with a grin. Then he thought about it again. "But that's equivalent to £250 per month! Are you telling me that it will cost Andycabs £250 per month just to use the car, without the cost of fuel, maintenance and tyres?"

I pointed out that it would be 'using up' the car during this period, rather than just using it, and gave him a moment or two to digest that idea while I made us another pot of tea, with biscuits this time.

Andrew wasn't sure that this was the most realistic way of doing things. He wondered if it might be simplifying things a bit too much to spread the cost of the car and fittings equally over the five years during which Andycabs expected to use them. That seemed to ignore some of the basic facts of life. For instance, the **book value** of the car will be reduced to (£20,000 –

£3,000 =) £17,000 at the end of the first year, but Andrew was sure that Andycabs would not be able to sell it for that sort of money, after having had one full year's use out of it. It would probably be lucky to get £10,000 – let alone £17,000. He then realised that the only way to reduce the value of the car to £10,000 would be to charge £10,000 for depreciation, instead of the £3,000 that he currently had in mind. That would certainly hit the first year's profits so perhaps it wasn't such a bright idea, after all.

Perhaps it wasn't. The trouble was that he was confusing **book value** with **market value**. The net balance of £17,000 is the **written down book value** of the car at the end of the year; it is based on a number of subjective judgments that Andrew has to make. Starting with the actual purchase price, he has to estimate its anticipated working life and its trade–in price at the end of that period. Then he has to use this combination of estimates to calculate what the written down value of the car would be at intermediate points in this working life.

This has nothing to do with its market value at those times. It's just his estimate of calculating a fair charge for its use over its working life. It is known as the **straight line method of depreciation** and is the most common method used, possibly because it is the simplest to calculate, and the easiest to understand. It is not the only method, however. There is the **reducing balance method**, and the **sum of year's digits method** – both of which charge more in earlier years than later. To that extent, they may measure up more closely with Andrew's feelings about loss of market value, but I don't want to go into that here.

Andrew agreed with that and then asked me how to enter depreciation onto the spreadsheet. "Will it come off the car column and off the income one?"

"Well, it could but the original cost of the car would be lost, as would the accumulated amount of depreciation that had been charged over the years, both of which are valuable pieces of information.

"Why are they both valuable?" asked Andrew.

"Together they give an analyst an idea as to how old the asset is."

"Right" said Andrew "Let's open another column then."

And that was quite correct. We need another column to record accumulated depreciation and, as it is closely related to the car column, I suggested that we should put it next to it.

Figure 3.0 – The spreadsheet so far

		Car	Acc. Deprn	A/Cs Rec.		Cash	=	Share Cap.		Bank Loan	A/Cs Pay.			Income
5	Balance Sheet year 0	20,000				2,000	=	12,000		10,000				
6	Tax, insurance, etc.					−2,000	=							2,000
7	Advertising					−1,000	=							−1,000
8	Revenue – cash					48,000	=							48,000
9	Revenue – credit			12,000			=							12,000
10	Fuel costs						=				10,000			−10,000
11	Maintenance/Tyres						=				8,000			−8,000
12	Telephone					−2,400	=							−2,400
13	Loan interest					−700	=							−700
14	Trial balance	20,000		12,000		43,900	=	12,000		10,000	18,000			35,900
15	**Depreciation**		**−3,000**				=							**−3,000**

Andrew studied the spreadsheet carefully. "I can see that you have kept both pieces of information separate, but I am a bit unhappy about the depreciation column being a minus column on the assets side. Why have you placed it there?"

He had a good point. "It could be placed on the liabilities side to avoid the minus sign, but I think that it makes more sense to put it next to the column that is to be reduced by it, and to live with the minus sign."

"It does make good, logical sense" admitted Andrew, still studying the spreadsheet carefully. "What else do we need to record? What about the outstanding amounts in the accounts receivable and the accounts payable columns? How should we deal with those?"

Settling accounts

"Do you think Andycabs' credit customers will have settled all their outstanding amounts by the year end, and will it have paid the garage all that it owes it?" I asked.

"I doubt it very much. There will be some balances in both of those columns."

The question is, how much. Andrew has already said that Andycabs will expect its accounts receivable customers to settle their accounts within a matter of weeks, rather than months, and the same principle will also apply to its accounts payable suppliers.

"What would happen if Andycabs failed to settle its fuel and maintenance accounts within a reasonable time?" I asked.

"I know jolly well what would happen." Andrew replied emphatically "Geoff Marsden would stop supplying it with fuel."

"You bet he would" I agreed "so time is the crucial element here, too. Now let's consider what you expect the outstanding balances to be for Andycabs' accounts receivable and accounts payable at the end of the year, and then we can work out how much Andycabs will have received and paid in order to arrive at those balances. Then we can enter them into the spreadsheet. Remember Andrew, accounts receivable settlements affect the lifeblood – cash – of the business and you must control the time they take to pay very carefully. Equally, as you just agreed, the business must pay its bills in a reasonable time in order to get continued reliable service from its suppliers."

Andrew paused and thought for a bit. "Well, according to my forecasts its total accounts receivable and accounts payable transactions during the first year will come to £12,000, and £18,000, respectively. Most of these debts will be cleared as the year goes by." After a little more thought and a bit of scribbling on a piece of paper, he suggested that the accounts receivable balances at the end of the year might come to about £1,300, and there would still be £1,800 owing to accounts payable. "So it will expect to receive £10,700 and to pay £16,200 from, and to, its accounts receivable and accounts payable respectively."

That seemed reasonable, so I asked him to enter these transactions onto the spreadsheet.

Figure 3.1 – Recording the settling of accounts

		Car	Acc. Deprn	A/Cs Rec.	Cash	=	Shane Cap,		Bank Loan	A/Cs Pay.	Income
14	Trial balance	20,000		12,000	43,900	=	12,000		10,000	18,000	35,900
15	Depreciation		−3,000			=					−3,000
16	**Cash from A/Cs Rec.**			−10,700	10,700	=					
17	**Cash to A/Cs Pay.**				−16,200	=				−16,200	

Andrew soon completed these entries. "What's next?" he asked.

"Now we have to consider whether Andycabs will have to make any payments in the current year for services it will receive in the following year." I replied.

Prepayments and accruals

As the name implies, prepayments are payments Andycabs will make before it uses up the goods or services involved. If these goods or services are used up before the end of this financial year, they will be charged to the income column as expenses in this year. If they are not to be used up until the next year however, they will be assets and, as such, will be in its closing balance sheet. They will not affect the current year's income, of course, although they will certainly affect its cash balance.

"I agree that they are assets but are they 'operating assets' though?" asked Andrew.

"Yes they are, because they enable Andycabs to trade and earn revenues in the coming year," I replied.

The road tax, insurance and licence fees for Andycabs' second year come under this heading because they will have to be paid before the end of Year 1. He had suggested £2,000 for these costs in Year 1, so by the very nature of things, it seems sensible to assume that they might well increase to £2,100 in Year 2.

"OK. Let's get that into the spreadsheet" said Andrew, encouraged by the fact that I was not suggesting anything likely to reduce the income column.

Figure 3.2 – Allowing for prepayments

		Car	Ace. Deprn	A/Cs Rec.	Prepayments	Cash	=	Share Cap,	Bank Loan	A/Cs Pay.	Income
14	Trial balance	20,000		12,000		43,900	=	12,000	10,000	18,000	35,900
15	Depreciation		–3,000				=				–3,000
16	Cash from A/ Cs Rec.			–10,700		10,700	=				
17	Cash to A/Cs Pay.					–16,200	=			–16,200	
18	**Prepayments**				**2,100**	**–2,100**	=				

Accrued expenses are the opposite of prepayments. They refer to the fact that Andycabs will be making use of goods and services for which its suppliers have not charged it by its year end. For example, gas, electricity and telephone accounts are submitted after the end of the periods to which they relate, simply because these billing companies cannot charge their customers until they know how much they have used. Andycabs will have had the benefit of them though, which means that they have to be charged to the income column as expenses. That is only fair; expenses for which the invoices have not yet been received have to be estimated and included.

Andrew looked concerned. "But what if you get your estimate wrong, and when the invoice arrives it is for a different amount? Say Andycabs charged this year's income column with £400 for a telephone bill, my best estimate, but next year it received an invoice for £450?"

This often happens. After all, one can't always make accurate predictions of the unseen bills. It has to be a judgment of the likely amount.

Andrew was reluctant to let this go. "Wouldn't this mean that the extra £50 will have to be charged in the following year? And then, in that case, wouldn't it also mean that both this year's and next year's profits will both be wrong in some way?"

"Yes, it does" I agreed "but this just emphasises that the eventual profit figure is the outcome of a series of best judgments. It's the same problem that we had with the depreciation charge, which was also based on the estimates that you made about the car's useful lifespan and its disposal value, wasn't it?" When Andrew admitted that this was true, I repeated that the profit figure is derived from the best set of estimates made in the circumstances.

"I see" Andrew replied, "well, I think we should consider that my estimates of costs already include any accruals. I agree that the accounts payable column should actually be called *accounts payable and accruals*, but that's such a mouthful, let's stick to accounts payable. I agree that I should split some of these forecasts into cash and accrual amounts, but it seems a bit pedantic to me, since we are dealing with the big picture, so let's ignore them."

I agreed, so from now on, when you see a column headed accounts payable, remember that it actually includes accruals as well. The same is true for the accounts receivable column as well; it includes accruals too, because Andycabs has to include estimated revenues for work that it has completed but for which it has not yet charged its customers.

Andrew was still worried about these accruals, and he asked me "I really would like you to show me, on a spreadsheet, how you would make these accrual entries, it would make the subject much clearer."

So here they are:

Figure 3.3 – Recording accruals

| YEAR | ASSETS | | = | LIABILITIES | | |
	Telephone Bill	Cash	=	A/Cs Pay.	Accruals	Income
YEAR 1	Not yet received		=		400	–400
YEAR 2	Bill received		=	450	–400	–50
YEAR 2	Bill settled	–450	=	–450		

"OK" said Andrew "That makes it much clearer. I'm a bit shocked at the way the profit figures of both years would be wrong, so to speak, but I see it is inevitable."

What's in it for me?

Andrew had been extremely patient, but he was unable to contain himself any longer. "Surely we have got to the point when we can record what Andycabs will be paying me? I don't mind if we have to revise it later, but let's get a figure in now."

Why not? Andrew said he would like to have a salary of £20,000 a year, so let's start with that.

"The tax authorities will want a part of your wages too, remember, and the company is responsible for deducting that part and then paying it to them."

"Hmm, then I will deduct £20,000 from the income column but only get part of it in cash – let's say the tax people want 20%, then I will get £16,000, and they will eventually get £4,000. Until they do they are an account payable, I suppose."

They are, but such an important one they get their very own column. This column can deal with all tax matters; it is called **Tax & PAYE**. PAYE is a shortening of *Pay As You Earn*, and it refers to the way tax is deducted by the company from the salaries of its employees every month. Since PAYE has to be paid monthly to the tax authorities, this column should be placed to the right of the accounts payable one. In America payroll taxes are dealt with in the same way.

The first part of the transaction made Andrew scratch his head a bit. "Look" he said, "I have taken

£20,000 from the income column, put £4,000 in a new column called as you just suggested, 'Tax and PAYE', and taken £16,000 from the cash column. It balances all right but now I've got three entries on one line, that's something new."

"That's no problem Andrew; as long as the line balances you can have more than two entries if necessary. When there are more than two, financial people often write a little note to remind them why they did so, called a **journal entry**. The journal is very useful for recording unusual types of transactions."

Figure 3.4 – Andrew enters his salary and pays the tax authorities their share

		Car	Ac. De-prn	A/Cs Rec.	Prepay-ments	Cash	=	Share Cap,	Bank Loan	A/Cs Pay,	Tax & PAYE	Income
14	Trial balance	20,000		12,000		43,900	=	12,000	10,000	18,000		35,900
15	Depreciation		−3,000				=					−3,000
16	Cash from A/Cs Rec,			−10,700		10,700	=					
17	Cash to A/Cs Pay.					−16,200	=			−16,200		
18	Prepayments				2,100	−2,100	=					
19	**Salary**					**−16,000**	=				**4,000**	**−20,000**
20	**Pay PAYE**					**−4,000**	=				**−4,000**	

Suitably reassured Andrew carried on, including recording the payment to the tax people, and he gave a sigh of relief because, when he added up the income column, he saw that there was still a positive balance. "Ah. That's all right then. Have we nearly finished now?"

"Nearly, yes, but still not quite."

It looks fairly obvious that Andycabs will have positive cash balances in the bank, so we should calculate the likely interest these will earn. This will depend in practice upon the day-to-day balances that are in the bank account, but we need an estimate for the whole year. To get this let's assume that the sum of the cash flows, before calculating the interest received, will be in the bank, on average, for 50% of the time. Applying this method and multiplying the result by the rate of interest it will receive, we get an amount of £100. Andrew was quick to enter this in the spreadsheet.

Entering the Interest Received

"Hmm, it is interest earned so it will increase Andycabs' assets and, as the company must owe that to us, its shareholders, it must go into income column. I've got to remember that we are including the bank balances in the cash account. You told me earlier that cash is a facilitator and does not earn anything itself, so I must remember that the interest earned is actually on the amounts in the bank, not on cash in the business." And he was right again.

Figure 3.5 – The interest calculation and entry

		Car	Ace. Deprn	A/Cs Rec,	Prepay-ments	Cash	=	Share Cap,	Bank Loan	A/Cs Pay,	Tax & PAYE	Income
14	Trial balance	20,000		12,000		43,900	=	12,000	10,000	18,000		35,900
15	Depreciation		−3,000				=					−3,000
16	Cash from A/Cs Rec,			−10,700		10,700	=					
17	Cash to A/Cs Pay.					−16,200	=			−16,200		
18	Prepayments				2,100	−2,100	=					
19	Salary					−16,000	=				4,000	−20,000
20	Pay PAYE					−4,000	=				−4,000	
21	**Interest received**					**100**	=					**100**

This brings us to **provisions**, but before considering the one that is relevant to Andycabs (the tax provision) first let's look at the topic more widely.

Provisions

Unfortunately, many companies find that some of their accounts receivable customers fail to pay their bills. They do not know which customers will not pay, but experience leads them to expect that a certain percentage of them will fall into this category. The 'true and fair view' principle requires that these **bad debts** are charged to the income column in the year the sale was made. But, since, at their year-end, companies do not know which of their customers will not pay it is usual for them to estimate a percentage of the accounts receivable balance and to charge that against income.

Although such a **provision** is charged against the income statement, the last thing companies want to do is to let any of their accounts receivable customers know that they do not expect them to pay what they owe. As long as there is still some hope of eventual payment, the best thing to do is leave the accounts receivable column as it is and to find another home to balance this transaction. "Like a new column" as Andrew was quick to suggest "I don't think we should include this in our plans for Andycabs, but please show me how to enter such things in a spreadsheet."

Figure 3.6 – Recording provisions

		ASSETS		=	LIABILITIES	
		Acs/rec.	Cash	=	Provisions	Income
1	Initial provision in anticipation that this amount of all a/cs receivable will never be paid made in year 1			=	100	−100
2	Eventual write off of an particular account receivable in year 2	−30		=	−30	
3	Unexpected receipt from that account maybe in year 3		30	=		30

By providing for a possible loss of revenue, Andycabs would charge this loss in the current year, but the accounts receivable column would still show the full amount of outstanding debts. If, eventually, the decision is taken to write off a particular debt, then that will be the time to deduct it from both accounts receivable and provisions.

Even after this has been done, maybe, one day, the bill will be paid. If this happens, Andycabs could not deduct it from the accounts receivable column, because the original entry will have been eliminated already, as shown in figure 3.6. Instead, cash will be increased by the amount received, and the balancing entry will be in the income column and described as 'unexpected revenue'.

The use of provisions is not confined to providing for bad debts though; other things might need to be provided for too.

Andrew was rather intrigued by all this. "What is the difference between an accrual and a provision then; they seem to mean similar things, and what other things might companies have to provide for?"

An accrual is related to goods or services that have been received or used by the company, but for which no invoice has arrived. Even so these invoices are of a predictable amount and are sure to arrive. There is an inevitability about them that does not always apply to provisions. For example, where there is a legal action in progress against a company it might be years before the outcome is known. If the company is concerned that the judgment may go against it, it will estimate what it might cost and provide for that amount by charging it against income, just in case. This is a typical provision. It reduces the income of the period in which the need for it first became apparent, thus ensuring that the correct period gets charged, as long as we get our estimate right.

"Remember, Andrew, such provisions do not affect cash, of course."

"Yes, but what happens if it doesn't get its estimate right?" asked Andrew.

"If the provision turns out to have been too small, then the extra is charged against income in the year when this becomes known. If it is more than enough, then income benefits from the difference"

"Ah, but this means that the income made in both years will be wrong again, maybe by a large amount."

"That's true, Andrew. Companies tend to provide for their worst estimate in the first place, then if they do get it wrong, the adjustment they will have to make will be a benefit to income, not a charge."

"I don't think Andycabs should provide for any bad debts. Are there any provisions that it has to make?"

"Yes, there is one; it has to provide for the tax it will have to pay on this year's profit, even though it may not have to pay it until next year and even though the tax people might well ask for a somewhat different figure."

This is true for all companies who, in order to prepare their financial statements in time for their **Annual General Meetings**, have to provide for their best estimates of the probable tax due. These estimates are unlikely to be the amounts that they will have to pay, and any adjustment will appear in their next year's income statements.

"You mentioned that Andycabs will have to pay tax too, a few minutes ago, not a pleasant thought. Do I just work out a percentage and deduct it from the income column – and when exactly does Andycabs have to pay it?" Andrew asked.

Working out the amount of tax a company has to pay is complicated and requires knowledge of tax law. The same is true for the amount of PAYE to deduct, but this is not the place to address those problems. Remember, this is not a tax textbook. I suggested to Andrew that he should charge 20% of the remaining profits, which was simple and which would produce a number for him to enter into the spreadsheet. Then I suggested that he should round it up to make it easier for us to use. I also told him that Andycabs will not have to pay it until the next year. *[Note: This is the simplest assumption; countries differ in the periods in which they require tax to be paid]*

"OK, I'll do that. By the way, most of Andycabs' revenues will be in cash, so how can the tax authorities be sure that I have included all of them as revenue, fares and tips, I mean?"

"It's a fair question Andrew. The tax authorities are always faced with a problem when cash revenues are involved. I had a look at their website (www.hmrc.gov.uk) to see if I could find out how they tackle it, but all it said was:

> 'This area of guidance has been withheld because disclosure would prejudice the assessment or collection of taxes/duties or assist tax/duty avoidance or evasion.'

So I cannot tell you, I can guess though; I expect they will compare Andycabs' profitability with that of other taxi firms in the town, and if it is much lower than theirs they may well base their tax calculation on a higher profit than Andycabs declared."

"What! That doesn't seem fair, if it really was making less profit."

"Who said life was fair Andrew? Where tax is concerned, I'm afraid the tax people will assume the worst, and it would be up to Andycabs to prove them wrong."

Suspense.

"I've got another question for you, Richard. What should I do if I know one of the columns to enter an item in, but I am not sure which other column I should use? I have to make two entries or my line will not balance."

"That's easily taken care of, by applying the golden rule, Andrew; *never get stuck, just open another column!* In this case it is called a **suspense** column. The entry can sit there until you learn where it should actually live and then you can transfer it. The suspense column has to be empty before Andycabs' financial statements are published or they would not show the 'true and fair view' that its shareholders require."

"Can you give me an example?" Andrew asked.

"Well, say a company receives an invoice which it recognises as legitimate, but it does not know which expense column is the relevant one. In this case, it will enter it in the suspense column until matters become clear."

This column is very useful. It allows problems to be recorded and yet held in abeyance until they are resolved.

The final entries

Returning to the spreadsheet, Andrew added up the income column, which came to £13,000 and decided to provide for £2,600, a little more than 20% – "To be on the safe side" he said.

"So, Andycabs will have a profit after tax of £10,400, and that's after paying me a salary of

£20,000, too. That's not too bad. In fact it looks pretty good to me."

"Hang on a minute, Andrew, you, its employee, will have to work hard for it to make those profits; you could have been earning at least £20,000 working for someone else and your capital of £12,000 would then still be earning interest."

Andrew thought about this for a while. "So there is another cost for working for Andycabs: I lose the opportunity of earning money working for someone else, and we lose the interest we could have earned on our £12,000. I remember Joan mentioning that some time ago. That does put another complexion on it I admit, but we are determined to own our own business and I am confident that Andycabs will, eventually, be able to pay me more than that. We'll take the risk."

That was a good analysis of the situation. What Andrew has done is to identify what is called the **Opportunity Cost** of their actions: what they might have received by taking another course of action:

Andrew soon brightened up again. "OK. Fair enough" he said "but that's if I only get 24,000 fare miles–worth of business. If I manage to clock up 30,000 fare miles, then Andycabs will probably make even more profits. What do we have to do now?"

"We have nearly finished, Andrew, but there is one more thing to think about, and that is Andycabs' dividend policy. If it is going to make a profit after tax of £10,400, and has the cash available, is it going to declare a dividend?"

"Hmm, dividends; yes indeed, let's declare a dividend of 40% of the profit that is left."

Why not? When a company declares a dividend it has to wait for its shareholders to approve it at the company's annual general meeting, which, as I have already mentioned, is held after the company's year-end. The dividend is declared as being an amount per share. Andrew's decision would yield a dividend of about £4,200, which would be expressed as thirty-five pence per share.

"So, Andrew, please make the entries for the tax and dividends."

The tax entry he found quite easy, as there was a 'Tax and PAYE' column already on the spreadsheet for him to use. Then, after a little thought, at least ten seconds worth, he decided to open another column on the liabilities side, called it 'Dividends', and entered £4,200 into it. He reasoned that tax would be paid before the dividends were, so he placed the dividend column to the left of the 'Tax and PAYE' column on the spreadsheet.

Figure 3.7 – Providing for tax and dividends

		Car	Acc. Deprn	A/Cs Rec.	Prepay-ments	Cash	=	Share Cap,	Bank Loan	A/Cs Pay.	Divi-dend	Tax & PAYE	Income
14	Trial balance	20,000		12,000		43,900	=	12,000	10,000	18,000			35,900
15	Depreciation		–3,000				=						–3,000
16	Cash from A/Cs Rec,			–10,700		10,700	=						
17	Cash to A/Cs Pay.					–16,200	=			–16,200			
18	Prepayments				2,100	–2,100	=						
19	Salary					–16,000	=					4,000	–20,000
20	Pay PAYE					–4,000	=					–4,000	
21	Interest received					100	=						100
22	Provision for tax						=					2,600	–2,600
23	Dividends declared						=				4,200		–4,200

When he had finished, I explained that he should now transfer the profit from the income column, to empty it, ready to be used in the next year.

"OK, I'll put a balancing entry into the share capital column then" he said.

"Oh no you won't" I replied "you can only put entries into that column when shares are issued."

"So what will I do with it then?"

"You can open a new column for it and call it **retained profits**, or **reserves**, if you like. It's sometimes called **accumulated income** too. Then you can complete the spreadsheet by adding up all the columns."

Andrew soon had the spreadsheet completed, putting the retained profit column next to the share capital one. "Andycabs still owes it to us" he said.

Notice that the most durable things are listed first and the most liquid items are listed last. The car column appears before the accounts receivable one which itself comes before the cash column. Similarly, long–term liabilities, such as share capital, retained profits, and long–term bank loan, appear before accounts payable etc. The income column is a temporary column, which records the year's revenues and expenses, and transferring its final balance to retained profits each year empties it.

Fig.3.8 The completed spreadsheet

	YEAR 1	Car	Acc. Deprn	A/Cs Rec.	Prepay-ments	Cash	=	Share Cap.	Ret Profit	Bank Loan	A/Cs Pay.	Divi-dend	Tax & PAYE	Income
1	Capital invested					12,000	=	12,000						0
2	Bank loan					10,000	=			10,000				0
3	Car purchase	18,000				-18,000	=							0
4	Car fittings	2,000				-2,000	=							0
5	Balance Sheet year 0	20,000	0	0	0	2,000	=	12,000	0	10,000	0	0	0	0
6	Tax, insurance, etc.					-2,000	=							-2,000
7	Advertising					-1,000	=							-1,000
8	Revenue - cash					48,000	=							48,000
9	Revenue - credit			12,000			=							12,000
10	Fuel costs						=				10,000			-10,000
11	Maintenance/Tyres						=				8,000			-8,000
12	Telephone					-2,400	=							-2,400
13	Loan interest					-700	=							-700
14	Trial balance	20,000	0	12,000	0	43,900	=	12,000	0	10,000	18,000	0	0	35,900
15	Depreciation		-3,000				=							-3,000
16	Cash from A/Cs Rec.			-10,700		10,700	=							0
17	Cash to A/Cs Pay.					-16,200	=				-16,200			0
18	Prepayments				2,100	-2,100	=							0
19	Salary					-16,000	=						4,000	-20,000
20	Pay PAYE					-4,000	=						-4,000	0
21	Interest received					100	=							100
22	Provision for tax						=						2,600	-2,600
23	Dividends declared						=					4,200		-4,200
24	**Dividends paid**					**0**	=					**0**		
25	**Transfer net profit**						=		6,200					-6,200
26	Balance Sheet year 1	20,000	-3,000	1,300	2,100	16,400	=	12,000	6,200	10,000	1,800	4,200	2,600	0
				36,800			=				36,800			

Andrew studied the spreadsheet closely, and said "Well! That was a lot easier than I thought it was going to be. Thank goodness both sides add up to the same totals, £36,800, it's a pretty nice feeling I can tell you. So where do we go from here?"

"Remember that I suggested that we should not use the expanded equation:

'Assets + Expenses = Liabilities + Revenues'

because it would involve too many columns if we did so, and it would not fit onto the page? Well, I think I should show you a summarised spreadsheet with just one column each for all expense items and one for all revenues, so that you know how the expanded system works. Here it is:

Figure 3.9 – The spreadsheet expanded to include and expense and a revenue column

	YEAR 1	Car	Acc. Depm	A/Cs Rec.	Pre-pay-ments	Exp-enses	Cash	=	Share Cap.	Ret Profit	Bank Loan	A/Cs Pay,	Divi-dend	Tax & PAYE	Rev-enues	Income
1	Capital invested						12,000	=	12,000							0
2	Bark loan						10,000	=			10,000					0
3	Car purchase	18,000					−18,000	=								0
4	Car fittings	2,000					−2,000	=								0
5	Balance Sheet year 0	20,000	0	0	0	0	2,000	=	12,000	0	10,000	0	0	0	0	0
6	Tax, insurance, etc.,					2,000	−2,000	=								0
7	Advertising					1,000	−1,000	=								0
8	Revenue – cash						48,000	=							48,000	0
9	Revenue – cred t			12,000				=							12,000	0
10	Fuel costs					10,000		=				10,000				0
11	Maintenance/Tyres					8,000		=				8,000				0
12	Telephone					2,400	−2,400	=								0
13	Loan interest					700	−700	=								0
14	Trial balance	20,000	0	12,000	0	24,100	43,900	=	12,000	0	10,000	18,000	0	0	60,000	0
15	Depreciation		−3,000			3,000		=								0
16	Cash from A/Cs Rec,			−10,700			10,700	=								0
17	Cash to A/Cs Pay.						−16,200	=				−16,200				0
18	Prepayments				2,100		−2,100	=								0
19	Salary					20,000	−16,000	=						4,000		0
20	Pay PAYE						−4,000	=						−4,000		0
21	Interest 'received						100	=							100	0
22	Trial balance	20,000	−3,000	1,300	2,100	47,100	16,400	=	12,000	0	10,000	1,800	0	0	60,100	0
23	Transfer expenses					−47,100		=								−47,100
24	Transfer revenues							=							−60,000	60,000
25	Transfer interest							=							−100	100
22	Provis on for tax							=						2,600		−2,600
23	Dividends declared							=					4,200			−4,200
24	Dividends paid						0	=					0			0
25	Transfer net profit							=		6,200						−6,200
26	Balance Sheet year 1	20,000	−3,000	1,300	2,100	0	16,400	=	12,000	6,200	10,000	1,800	4,200	2,600	0	0
				36,800				=				36,800				

Andrew examined it with interest. "There are no entries in the income column until after we get to line 22 and then all the expenses and revenue totals are transferred into it."

"That's true Andrew, that's because I didn't open columns for the individual items, if I had done so the spreadsheet would not have fitted onto the page. In practice they would all have their own columns. What else do you notice?"

"Well, the expense and revenue columns do not appear in the closing balance sheet, nor does the income column. Why is that?"

"It's because they are temporary columns, Andrew, essential for recording the detail that a business needs for accuracy and control, but always closed, first to the income column which is itself then closed to the retained profit column at the end of a trading period."

"So Richard, are we going to use this expanded spreadsheet from now on then?"

"No" I replied "I would rather we revert to the simpler version. I felt I should show you this one to complete the picture."

"Whew, thank goodness for that!" Andrew replied. "So, what comes next?"

I explained that we were now going to produce some financial statements that would tell us the stories behind the numbers: the income statement, the cash flow statement, and the balance sheet.

"That sounds difficult. It means a lot more work, I suppose?" Andrew blanched a bit, as we had been hard at it for several hours.

"No. We've already got all the figures we need on the spreadsheet in figure 3.8" I assured him "we can extract all those statements from it."

"Oh, come on," exclaimed Andrew, incredulously. "You're not asking me to believe that we can produce all those reports from just that one spreadsheet? You must be joking. Surely we can't produce a complete set of financial statements from it?"

"But it is true, Andrew and, in our next three meetings, we will see what stories they tell us. Remember what I told you earlier; **know your numbers, know your business**"

Summary

It was gone eleven pm when Andrew got home, but Joan was still up and keen to hear all the details of his evening's discussion.

"There is a lot to tell you" Andrew warned, "we will be up for hours."

"Why not make a start anyway, I'll tell you if I want you to leave some of it until tomorrow."

True and fair view

"Richard explained to me that all companies are required to present a 'true and fair view' of their trading positions at the end of each financial year, and that it is essential that they include the revenues and expenses of that year, irrespective of when cash is actually received or paid out. This means that movements in cash are not necessarily related to increases or decreases in profit, and he gave me some examples. The first of these referred to assets that have useful lives that will extend over several years and so the original costs of these assets need to be charged against income annually in a fair way. He called that charge 'depreciation'. He emphasised that cash is affected when those assets were paid for and that the annual depreciation charge does not affect cash. He explained that the cost of the car could also be viewed as being a large prepayment for benefits that will be created by it over its useful life. Thus, it is only fair to spread that cost over the years that it will create those benefits. He called it the 'matching principle'. I think it's easier to think of it as the cost of using up the car, though.

He moved on to sales and to purchases of expense items on credit that also create phasing differences. The income column would be increased by sales revenues and decreased by the cost of those purchases made in the period under review. The company's cash position, on the other hand, only changes as and when debts are actually settled, and this may well be in the next year or even later.

Businesses sometimes have to pay in advance for goods or services (such as rent, etc.). These are prepayments; cash is depleted in one year, but the income statement will not be charged until a later year.

Accrued expenses have the opposite effect. These are expenses charged against profit in respect of services used in that period, but for which bills have not yet been received. Cash, of course, will not be reduced until the next year.

The next three things we discussed were:

Provisions.

In Andycabs' case, it is necessary to provide for the impact of an eventual tax bill. An estimate is made and charged against the profits of the current period, although the payment will not be made until next year. *[Note: In practice it depends on the particular country's rule as to when it is to be paid]*

Suspense.

This column is used as a temporary home for items when it is uncertain as to where they should be entered. When this becomes clear they will be moved out of suspense and into their rightful columns.

Dividends.

The amount of available profits that will eventually be paid to the shareholders,

The need to produce financial statements that give a true and fair view of a company means that increases or decreases in its cash position hardly ever agree with the profit or loss it has made in the year. Cash and profit are not the same, and a misunderstanding of this has led to many business failures.

Then came opportunity cost. While I would be working hard to generate Andycabs' profit, I would be sacrificing the opportunity of earning a living from elsewhere. The amount of income that I might have earned, together with the interest that we could have earned on our capital, represent the opportunity cost of investing in, and working for, Andycabs. In the long run, the return we will receive from Andycabs – including the amount we might sell it for in the future, will, hopefully, be bigger than that which I could have received from adopting an alternative course of action. When I said to him …"

At this point, just as Andrew was bending down to extract his computer from its case, Joan said, "That's enough for tonight Andy, let's go to bed. You can tell me the rest tomorrow. You did cover a lot of ground today."

"A good idea, in fact, I'll include the rest in my summary of our next meeting."

CHAPTER FOUR

THE SPREADSHEET OVERVIEW AND THE INCOME STATEMENT STORY

Soon we will be extending the business plan
for a full five years of its future.

But now that all of the transactions have been
entered into the spreadsheet,
let's pause, and see what stories it holds,
starting with the Income Statement Story.

Also, Andrew wants to know how inventory would be recorded
and any sales taxes like VAT as well.

Introduction

A bird's eye view

Figure 4.0 - The completed spreadsheet

	YEAR 1	Car	Acc. Deprn	A/Cs Rec.	Prepay-ments	Cash	=	Share Cap.	Ret Profit	Bank Loan	A/Cs Pay.	Divi-dend	Tax & PAYE	Income
1	Capital invested					12,000	=	12,000						0
2	Bank loan					10,000	=			10,000				0
3	Car purchase	18.000				−18,000	=							0
4	Car fittings	2,000				−2,000	=							0
5	Balance Sheet year 0	20,000	0	0	0	2,000	=	12,000	0	10,000	0	0	0	0
6	Tax, insurance, etc.,					−2,000	=							−2,000
7	Advertising					−1,000	=							−1,000
8	Revenue = cash					48,000	=							48,000
9	Revenue = credit			12,000			=							12,000
10	Fuel costs						=				10,000			−10,000
11	Maintenance/Tyres						=				8,000			−8,000
12	Telephone					−2,400	=							−2,400
13	Loan interest					−700	=							−700
14	Trial balance	20,000	0	12,000	0	43,900	=	12,000	0	10,000	18,000	0	0	35,900
15	Depreciation		−3,000				=							−3,000
16	Cash from A/Cs Rec,			−10,700		10,700	=							0
17	Cash to A/Cs Pay.					−16,200	=				−16,200			0
16	Prepayments				2,100	−2,100	=							0
19	Salary					−16,000	=						4,000	−20,000
20	Pay PAYE					−4,000	=						−4,000	0
21	Interest received					100	=							100
22	Provision for tax						=						2,600	−2,600
23	Dividends declared						=					4,200		−4,200
24	Dividends paid					0	=					0		
25	Transfer net profit						=		6,200					=6,200
26	Balance Sheet year 1	20,000	−3,000	1,300	2,100	16,400	=	12,000	6,200	10,000	1,800	4,200	2,600	0
						36,800	=				36,800			

Andrew arrived at my office on the Thursday evening at about 18.30, as I had suggested. Having organised a jug of coffee and a plate of biscuits, we settled down around the conference table, and turned on our computers.

"Let's examine the completed spreadsheet in more detail Andrew. Notice in particular that the cash and income column entries are not always the same; sometimes an income column entry is balanced with a cash column one, and sometimes not. Look at their totals too, there is £16,400 in cash, and yet Andycabs is only able to transfer a profit of £6,200 to the retained profit column.

Andrew looked closely at the two columns "It's all to do with that fairness principle you were telling me about, isn't it? For example, it is only fair to recognise that Andycabs earns revenue when it carries a customer even though it is a contract customer and the money might not come in until after its year end."

"Yes" I replied "and, the fairness idea also means that we have to include accruals, provisions, and the depreciation charge too. These all reduce profits, but not cash. For example, cash will be reduced when you buy the car, but the income column will not be affected by that transaction.

The spreadsheet is an extremely powerful tool. So far we have only used it to record Andycabs' budget estimates for its first year, but we can use it to look forward for more years than that, the closing balance sheet of one spreadsheet becoming the opening one of the following year. What's more, if any of the original estimates are changed, this will revise the business plan for all five years instantly."

"Five years' plans? That sounds great, but I would rather see what stories this spreadsheet has for me before we start projecting into the future, please."

"Let's start with the income column then. This is Andycabs' financial history book; it summarises its trading transactions during the year. Where does this story begin?"

"No question about that" Andrew replied emphatically "it has to be the revenue figure. That's what drives the business, after all. Especially Andycabs' business" he added, looking up to make sure I hadn't missed the pun.

"After that, I'd deduct my salary and the fuel and maintenance costs, because they are the ones most directly related to the miles travelled. That would show me how much profit Andycabs had available to cover its other costs, like the road tax, licence fees, telephone costs and loan interest."

"So what will your statement look like, Andrew?"

It did not take Andrew very long to produce the statement shown in figure 4.1.

Figure 4.1 Andycabs Income Statement Story for Year 1

Revenue				
		Cash	48,000	
		Credit	12,000	60,000
Interest				100
Total				60,100
Driving Expenses				
		Salary	−20,000	
		Fuel	−10,000	
		Maintenance	−8,000	−38,000
Profit left				22,100
Other Expenses				
		Tax, Insurance, and		
		Licence Fees	−2,000	
		Advertising	−1,000	
		Telephone	−2,400	
		Depreciation	−3,000	
Loan Interest			−700	
Provision for tax			−2,600	
Dividends			−4,200	−15,900
Retained Profit				6,200

"There you are," he said, with a flourish, when he'd finished. "There's Andycabs' income statement story. It contains all the income column figures and adds up to the same total too."

"Yes, Andrew, it tells us a compelling story; we can see how much profit is left, after deducting driving expenses, to cover its other costs, and we can see the final profit too. But I think I can make it even more useful to you by putting in some different subtotals. In this way the **operating expenses** can be separated from the **financing** ones and from the **tax** charge."

Loan interest paid is regarded as a **financial expense**, not an operating one, because it is linked to the financing of the business, rather than to its trading operations. The same is mainly true about interest earned, which depends upon how much of Andycabs' cash is earning interest, although, admittedly, its operations created that cash in the first place.

Similarly, the **provision for taxation** depends on how much profit Andycabs has made. Finally, **dividends** are declared out of profits after this tax charge has been deducted, so we need a subtotal here too. After the dividends have been deducted we arrive at the **profit retained** in the business.

You can see this presentation in Figure 4.2. It is similar to Andrew's but the differences are significant. There is a group heading for direct expenses, and, inset, the detail figures. **Direct expenses**, or direct **costs** as they are also called, are those that have to be incurred in order to deliver the product or service. In Andycabs' case these will be the ones that actually keep the taxi rolling, his salary, the road tax and insurance on the car, the regulation examinations, the fuel, and the maintenance costs. Deducting these from sales revenue gives Andycabs' **gross operating margin**.

The principal differences between this version and Andrew's are easy to see. The names of the headings used are the more traditional ones used in the UK. (In America, overhead expenses are sometimes referred to as **burden**).

The different levels of profit that are identified are useful for different reasons, in particular; the profit before interest paid and tax (PBIT), profit before tax (PBT), and profit after tax (PAT), as explained below:

PBIT shows how well the operations of a business have performed, regardless of how it is financed. It is an operating result.

PBT is the figure on which tax has to be paid (after adjustments made by the tax authorities that need not concern us here – remember, this is certainly not a tax textbook).

PAT is the point where Andycabs says to its shareholders (in this case, Andrew and Joan) "OK. This is the net amount of profit I've made for you over the year, and it's now up to you to decide whether the amount I am suggesting paying to you as dividends is what you want, leaving me with the rest to reinvest in the business."

In other words, the shareholders at the company's annual general meeting can either vote to accept the proposals of their directors to pay them dividends or not; it is rare for them to reject such a proposal!

Figure 4.2 - Andycabs' Income Statement story for the Year ended 31st March Year 1

Revenue	**Cash**		**48,000**
	Credit		**12,000**
			60,000
Direct expenses:			
Salary		−20,000	
Tax, insurance and licence fees		−2,000	
Fuel		−10,000	
Maintenance etc.		−8,000	−40,000
Gross Operating Profit			**20,000**
Overhead expenses			
Advertising		−1,000	
Telephone		−2,400	
Depreciation		−3,000	−6,400
Profit before all interest & tax			**13,600**
Non − operating income			100
Profit before interest payable and tax (PBIT)			13,700
Loan interest			−700
Profit before tax (PBT)			**13,000**
Provision for taxation @ 20%			−2,600
Profit after tax (PAT)			**10,400**
Dividends			−4,200
Retained profits			**6,200**

Andrew looked at this presentation and readily agreed that it told a more intriguing story than his own. "It puts the flesh on the bones, so to speak, and lets me focus on such things as the level of Andycabs' gross profit after the deduction of direct costs; the amount that its operational costs add up to, as distinct from the financial costs and the tax charges, and so on. Great, I feel I am beginning to identify the numbers that will help me run the business more effectively.

Let me summarise this story then, to see that I have got it right. It is our first story of business; it's Andycabs' financial history book. The story starts with sales revenue, and then we see the succeeding groups of expenses that it will have to incur in order to earn that revenue, and which will reduce its profits. We see the amount that it will have to be pay to the providers of outside finance, and to the tax authorities. Finally, we see how much it will pay to its shareholders and how much will be retained to give it **growth**. How about that?" He added the final question with his customary flourish and swallowed his (now cold) coffee in one gulp.

Notice that we have both used minus signs in our presentations. This was logical, since they had been used in the spreadsheets. In many published statements they are often left out, and the reader is expected, using common sense, to see whether an item increased or decreased profit. Fair enough, but if using minus signs makes things easier to understand, then let's use them.

Inventory and Sales Taxes (VAT in the UK)

"There are a couple of things that are worrying me a bit though," said Andrew "I don't have any inventory (A stock of potential customers would be nice) but how does the system deal with it in, for example, a retail shop and, as a business's revenue gets beyond a certain size, sales taxes, like value added tax, come into the picture. How are these dealt with?

"OK, Andrew, it is a good idea to generalise at this point. I doubt whether inventory will ever be a topic for you to worry about, but sales taxes like VAT might be one day, as you get bigger.

Let's ignore sales taxes to begin with. Here is a scenario for us to examine:

A retailer invests £1,000 in his shop. The shop then buys inventory for £400 on credit. It then sells £250 worth of this inventory for £600, again, on credit. Eventually the purchasers pay half of what they owe and the shop pays half of what it owes to its suppliers. There are no other transactions, costs, or revenues, so the shop now calculates how much profit it has made and transfers this to the owners retained profits column. The spreadsheet looks like this:

Figure 4.3 – Dealing with inventory

		Inven-tory	Cost of goods sold	A/Cs Rec.	Cash	=	Share Cap.	Ret. Profit	A/Cs Pay,	Rev-enue	In-come
1	Capital invested				1,000	=	1,000				
2	Buy inventory	400				=			400		
3	Sell inventory that cost 250 for £600			600		=				600	
4	Cost of goods sold	–250	250			=					
5	Trial balance	150	250	600	1,000	=	1,000	0	400	600	0
6	A/Cs receivable received			–300	300	=					0
7	Pay A/Cs payable				-200	=			–200		
8	Subtotal	150	250	300	1,100	=	1,000	0	200	600	0
9	Transfer revenue					=				–600	600
10	Transfer cost of goods sold to income		–250			=					–250
11	Transfer profit					=		350			–350
12	Closing Balance Sheet	150	0	300	1,100	=	1,000	350	200	0	0

Andrew studied this spreadsheet with great interest. "Please explain 'cost of goods sold to me" he said.

"As well as recording the sale of the goods for £600 we have to reduce the inventory column by the cost of those goods, otherwise we would be overstating the inventory in the closing balance sheet. So we open a new column called 'cost of goods sold'. When we want to calculate what profit the shop has made we transfer both the revenue and the cost of goods sold items into the income column. Finally we transfer the profit into the retained profits column. We record the payments made and then total the columns to give the closing balance sheet. Note that the temporary revenue, expense and income columns are empty now."

"Wow, that spreadsheet is so powerful isn't it? It's so easy to understand. Right, now show me how VAT is dealt with please."

"You won't be surprised to know that we deal with that by adding a new column, Andrew. Let's say VAT is levied at a rate of 20%. Then the goods bought will cost £400 + £80 = £480 and the accounts receivable will be £600 + £120 = £720. The spreadsheet now becomes:

Figure 4.4 – Dealing with Sales Taxes – VAT

		Inven-tory	Cost of goods sold	A/Cs Rec.	Cash		Share Cap.	Ret. Profit	A/Cs Pay.	VAT	Rev-enue	In-come
1	Capital invested				1,000	=	1,000					
2	Buy inventory	400				=			480	−80		
3	Sell inventory that cost 250 for £600			720		=				120	600	
4	Cost of goods sold	−250	250			=						
5	Trial balance	150	250	720	1,000	=	1,000		480	40	600	
6	A/Cs receivable received			−360	360	=						0
7	Pay A/Cs payable				−240	=			−240			
8	Pay VAT				−40	=				−40		
9	Subtotal	150	250	360	1,080	=	1,000	0	240	0	600	0
10	Transfer revenue										−600	600
11	Transfer cost of goods sold to income		−250			=						−250
12	Transfer profit					=		350				−350
13	Closing Balance Sheet	150	0	360	1,080	=	1,000	350	240	0	0	0

"I see" said Andrew "you have separated the VAT amounts from the original costs and revenues that impact on the shop and put them in their own column, so the shop's figures are all exclusive of VAT, including its profit. I see that the shop owes the tax people £120 but that it can deduct the VAT it suffered on its purchase, so it only has to pay them the difference, £40. Yes, that is all clear to me now. I have another question though, what if it wasn't a shop but a manufacturing company, converting raw materials into inventory for sale?"

"Hang on Andrew, don't get carried away! I think we have covered enough for this evening, tomorrow we can move on to the cash flow story."

Summary

"You're earlier this evening Andy" said Joan "I'm sorry that I had to stop you last night, but it was getting terribly late."

"Actually, it was a good place for me to stop, because now I can begin from where I got to last time. Hang on a minute, while I set up my laptop, then I can show you my spreadsheet. I still find it almost unbelievable that all of my budget estimates are on this one spreadsheet!"

Joan studied the spreadsheet carefully and commented that she had never seen financial figures presented in this way. "Is Richard going to explain to you how this ties in with the sort of accounts that I have to keep?" she asked.

"Well, he tells me that he is. Apparently the spreadsheet and the equation approach is an easier and more comprehensive way of explaining the principles than the way he was taught in his day."

"So, what did you do next, Andy?"

"Richard asked me to compare the cash and income columns and he explained why they were not the same. It's all to do with timing differences and the need to tell a 'true and fair' view of a company's affairs at its year-end. Then he asked me to rearrange the figures in the income column to make it tell a story about Andycabs' progress. I did, and it showed me how Andycabs had arrived at the final profit figure. I started with the sales revenue figure and deducted the expenses incurred in arriving at it. Then I deducted the amounts owing to the tax authorities, to the lenders and to shareholders. It was an extremely interesting story, rather like reading a history book. Richard then rearranged it to make it even more informative.

The income statement, the cash flow statement, and the balance sheet all present the financial life of a company in different ways, but they all share a common source of data - the transaction spreadsheet. Richard said that a report could be based on any column in the spreadsheet but that the most important columns are the income and cash columns. We are going to look at the cash flow story, at our next meeting.

I asked Richard to explain how a company like a shop would deal with inventory and sales taxes and he produced a couple more spreadsheets that made it very clear. That spreadsheet approach is very powerful, you know."

With that Andrew, looking very pleased with himself, asked whether, having sung for his supper, could he have it now please? Joan laughed, and told him that it was all ready and waiting in the oven.

CHAPTER FIVE

THE CASH FLOW STORY

Cash Flow is the second member of the trilogy
and a very important one too.

How should it be presented
to make it tell an informative story?

For a company, cash is its lifeblood –
lose too much of it and it will probably die.

Figure 5.0 – Cash entries only

1	Capital Invested	12,000
2	Bank loan	10,000
3	Car purchase	–18,000
4	Car fittings	–2,000
5	Balance Sheet Year 0	2,000
6	Tax, insurance, etc.	–2,000
7	Advertising	–1,000
8	Revenue = cash	48,000
9	Revenue = credit	0
10	Fuel costs	0
11	Maintenance/Tyres	0
12	Telephone	–2,400
13	Loan interest	–700
14	Trial balance	43,900
15	Depreciation	0
16	Cash from A/Cs Rec.	10,700
17	Cash to A/Cs Pay.	–16,200
18	Prepayments	–2,100
19	Salary	–16,000
20	Pay PAYE	–4,000
21	Interest received	100
22	Provision for tax	0
23	Dividends declared	0
24	Transfer net profit	0
25	Balance Sheet Year 1	16,400

Introduction

Having studied the story that the income statement told him, Andrew was keen to find out what the cash flow story might add and he arrived promptly at 18.30 pm. as agreed yesterday. After coffee we were ready to begin.

Sorting out the details

The transaction spreadsheet includes every forecast transaction up to the end of Andycabs' first year, including the setting–up transactions. These relate to Andrew's initial capital investment, the bank loan, and the purchase of the car and fittings. In other words, its story started from the very first line of the spreadsheet, whereas the income statement story (Figure 4.2) started at line six.

"So what do you make of that Andrew? What story can you get from the cash column?"

"Well, this is a bit more difficult than the income story" he replied, rubbing his chin. "Some of the outflows in this column refer to expenditures on operating items, and some to longer–term investments. Some are direct cash payments, and some are payments to suppliers (accounts payable). The same is true for the cash inflows; some come from the shareholders and the bank, some come from cash customers, while others come in as payments from contract customers (accounts receivable). I can see that I shall need to keep a very careful eye on all of this, but it seems to be a bit of a muddle.

Anyway, I suppose the first thing to decide is whether to start from the beginning, or from when Andycabs starts trading. If I start from the beginning, I'll have to include the issue of shares in return for £12,000 cash, and the bank loan of £10,000, and the money spent on the car. Perhaps I should show both situations. Hmm, it's as if we have an introduction to the trading story, isn't it? If the first part of Andycabs' cash flow story starts with the opening balances in Line 5 of the spreadsheet, then the setting–up transactions will form an introduction to it, like this"

Figure 5.2 The Andycabs' Cash Flow story

Operating cash flows			
	Revenue – cash	48,000	
	Cash from A/Cs Receivable	10,700	
		58,700	
Operating cash outflows			
	Tax, insurance, etc.	–2,000	
	Advertising	–1,000	
	Telephone	–2,400	
	Cash to suppliers	–16,200	
	Prepayments	–2,100	
	Salary	–16,000	
	Pay tax on salary	–4,000	–43,700
Gross cash from opns.			15,000
Financial income			100
Cash available			15,100
Financial charges			
	Dividends paid	0	
	Tax paid	0	
	Bank interest paid	–700	–700
Increase in cash			14,400

Figure 5.1 The Andycabs' Cash Flow story – introduction

Sources		
From Andrew		12,000
From the Bank		10,000
Total		22,000
Less uses		
Bought car	–18,000	
Bought fittings	–2,000	
Total		–20,000
Cash Remaining		2,000

"Right" said Andrew "now I will I write the rest of the story."

"There" he said, when he'd finished "cash is a story that I really do understand. It's similar to the income story, but it looks at things from a different angle" he turned his computer round so I could see better.

"As you can see, I have grouped the various sections into self– contained sets, each of which are inset. I like this idea, because the subtotals tell their own stories. Now I know it is a forecast, but let's assume that Andycabs does actually achieve these figures. Then the first section tells me how much money came in during its first year.

That's the most fascinating part, and it starts with the money received from its customers, both the cash paying ones and the amounts actually paid by its contract account customers too. Of course, this does not equal the total they owe Andycabs; it's just how much they have paid to date.

Similarly, I don't expect this story to tell me the total of Andycabs' purchases from its suppliers. It only deals with how much it pays them during the year, and I can see that clearly in the next section. The cash purchases come first, followed by the amounts paid to credit suppliers. Next comes my salary – looks quite a high figure when you see it in context here. When I total it all up and deduct this from the total cash inflow, I can see that Andycabs generated £15,000 from its operations.

Next we see that it will receive £100 in interest, giving it £15,100 in total. Then we come to **financial charges**. I have put in headings for dividends and tax, but Andycabs doesn't have to pay these until next year, so the entries are zero – I suppose next year I shall need lines on the spreadsheet to record these payments. Anyway, when I deduct the loan interest that will have to be paid, I see that Andycabs will end up with an extra £14,400 to add to the £2,000 that is in the bank. That seems a great result, to me. I feel a bit like one of Agatha Christie's detectives, tying up the loose ends in one of her novels."

Profit and Cash

"That's exactly what you are" I agreed "a detective. So why does the income statement story show a retained profit of £6,200, while the cash flow story shows a cash balance of £16,400, as shown in Figure 5.3: that is, it's opening balance of £2,000 plus the increase in cash of £14,400?"

His grin faded for a moment, but he soon recovered. "Ah, yes" he said, "I think I can cope with this one. It's all to do with this business of presenting a fair profit for the year, regardless of the actual cash movements that are taking place. In order to calculate the profit for a period, I have to deduct its expenses from its revenues. However, those revenues and expenses may not necessarily be the same as the receipts and payments that actually take place during the period. If they're not, then the profit figure is bound to be different from the change in the cash balance."

He was off to a flying start. Turning to his computer, he poised his pencil over the income and cash columns. "There you are," he said "the initial four transactions deal with the setting up of the business. We dealt with them as an introduction and they do not affect income at all. The first ones that do so are the road tax and insurance, the advertising and the cash revenues. They all affect both the income and the cash columns too.

The next three items, credit revenues, and credit purchases all affect the income column but have no immediate influence on cash. That will happen when the accounts are settled. The telephone and loan interest payments both come directly out of cash, and they affect both columns. That takes me down to the trial balance in Line 14. Then I come to the big one, depreciation. This is £3,000 of revenue expense that has nothing to do with cash, because the cash outlay was made when the car was purchased. Then we have the cash only transactions involved in payments and prepayments, then my salary and the tax on it, both of which affect income and cash in the year too. The noncash provisions for tax and for dividends come next, and then the transfer of the final profit figure to the retained profit column. In fact," he concluded, "it's all there on the spreadsheet, and the more I get used to that idea, the easier it becomes to see all these relationships at a glance. You couldn't possibly get the complete story from any of the independent single–dimensional statements, could you? You have to read them all to see what's going on."

He helped himself to another biscuit, and concluded that everything was fitting together nicely, thank you very much.

Figure 5.3 - Comparing the cash and income columns

	YEAH 1	Car	Ace. Deprn	A/Cs Rec.	Prepay-ments	Cash	=	Share Cap,	Pet Profit	Bank Loan	A/Cs Pay,	Divi-dend	Tax & PAYE	Income
1	Capital invested					12,000	=	12,000						0
2	Bank loan					10,000	=			10,000				0
3	Car purchase	18,000				−18,000	=							0
4	Car fittings	2,000				−2,000	=							0
5	Balance Sheet year 0	20,000	0	0	0	2,000	=	12,000	0	10,000	0	0	0	0
6	Tax, insurance, etc.					−2,000	=							−2,000
7	Advertising					−1,000	=							−1,000
8	Revenue = cash					48,000	=							48,000
9	Revenue = credit			12,000			=							12,000
10	Fuel costs						=				10,000			−10,000
11	Maintenance/Tyres						=				8,000			−8,000
12	Telephone					−2,400	=							−2,400
13	Loan interest					−700	=							−700
14	Trial balance	20,000	0	12,000	0	43,900	=	12,000	0	10,000	18,000	0	0	35,900
15	Depreciat on		−3,000				=							−3,000
16	Cash from A/Cs Rec,			−10,700		10,700	=							0
17	Cash 10 A/Cs Pay.					−16,200	=				−16,200			0
18	Prepayments				2,100	−2,100	=							0
19	Salary					−16,000	=						4,000	−20,000
20	Pay PAYE					−4,000	=						−4,000	0
21	Interest received					100	=							100
22	Provis on for tax						=						2,600	−2,600
23	Div dends declared						=					4,200		−4,200
24	Div dends pa d					0	=					0		0
25	Transfer net profit						=		6,200					−6,200
26	Balance Sheet year 1	20,000	−3,000	1,300	2,100	16,400	=	12,000	6,200	10,000	1,800	4,200	2,600	0
				36,800			=				36,800			

As Andrew has said, it all comes back to the over–riding need to be *fair* that was discussed at length in Chapter 3, where we saw that the revenues and expenses relating to that year have to be included, whether cash has moved or not. This is standard practice; it ensures that the published financial statements of a company present a true and fair view of its financial position at a given date.

It is called the **accrual convention**, or, in America, the **matching principle**; the only way to know how much profit a company has made is to deduct its expenses, including non–cash ones such as depreciation, from its revenues for that period. Auditors have to sign a declaration to the effect that, *to the 'best of their knowledge and belief'* this requirement has been satisfied.

Profit is not the same thing as cash, and they should never be confused. The profit made during a year will almost inevitably be different from the net amount of cash flowing in from trading operations, due to phasing differences between the two. Therefore, it is quite possible for a business to make losses, and still have sufficient cash to keep going for some time. Even more frightening is that a business can be making profits and yet still fail for lack of cash.

Andrew's bank manager will be very interested in these stories too; Andrew couldn't just turn up and ask for £10,000; he would need some forecasts to support such a request. A few notes scribbled on the back of an envelope to show that his cash receipts might be something in the region of..... and his outlays ought to be roughly....... wouldn't be good enough. The bank would want to satisfy itself that Andycabs is likely to grow sufficiently to pay back any money that it borrows.

"I think that's enough for this evening, Andrew. Let's meet again tomorrow and see what the balance sheet story has to tell us."

Summary

"I had a very good session this evening, Joan. The cash flow story was particularly interesting. It explains all the cash movements and shows how much cash Andycabs will generate, how much it will use and how much will be available for investment at the end of the year. Richard impressed upon me that profit and cash are not the same thing and that they should never be confused. The income statement story focuses on revenues and expenses, whilst the cash flow story is concerned with the amounts of cash received and cash spent. According to my estimates we will make a profit and have surplus cash at the end of the first year."

"That's great, Andy, what else did you learn?"

"Not much, actually, Richard told me that we would be looking at the balance sheet story tomorrow, and I am looking forward to that. I think it will be different to the other two because it does not appear in a column; it's the totals of all the columns instead. I wonder what we will make of it. I am looking forward to our next meeting, at 'The Foresters' for coffee on Saturday morning."

CHAPTER SIX

THE BALANCE SHEET STORY

This is the final member of the trilogy.

It differs from the other two
in that it shows a picture at a moment in time,
rather than telling a story about a period.

Being the oldest story of them all,
it has had lots of attention paid to it;
what should be in it,
how should it be arranged?

Introduction

It's always busy at 'The Foresters' on a Saturday, but as luck would have it, I was early enough to get a table outside on the lawn. It was a beautiful day and the forecast was set fair for the weekend. Andrew joined me soon afterwards, carrying his briefcase and his laptop.

"Why don't we stay here" he suggested, it's far too nice to go back to your office." It was, and I didn't need much persuasion, especially as Kathy had just brought out the coffees I had ordered.

"My, you two are always working these days" she said, greeting us with a smile. "No peace for the wicked" I replied.

"It's not that bad," protested Andrew, who just couldn't wait to tackle the third and final story. At least, that's what he told me.

"OK Andrew, take another look at the spreadsheet (in Figure 6.0), and tell me how you think that the balance sheet story will differ from both the income statement story and the cash flow story. Remember, those two stories both relate to a period, in this case a year, and they summarise the transactions that we expect to take place during that year. Is the balance sheet like that too, is it referring to a period of time as well?"

Figure 6.0 - The completed spreadsheet

	YEAR 1	Car	Acc. Deprn	A/Cs Rec,	Pre-pay-ments	Cash	=	Share Cap,	Ret Profit	Bank Loan	A/Cs Pay,	Divi-dend	Tax &PAYE	Income
1	Capital invested					12,000	=	12,000						0
2	Bank loan					10,000	=			10,000				0
3	Car purchase	18,000				−18,000	=							0
4	Car fittings	2,000				−2,000	=							0
5	Balance Sheet year 0	20,000	0	0	0	2,000	=	12,000	0	10,000	0	0	0	0
6	Tax, insurance, etc.,					−2,000	=							−2,000
7	Advertising					−1,000	=							−1,000
8	Revenue – cash					48,000	=							48,000
9	Revenue – credit			12,000			=							12,000
10	Fuel costs						=				10,000			−10,000
11	Maintenance/Tyres						=				8,000			−8,000
12	Telephone					−2,400	=							−2,400
13	Loan interest					−700	=							−700
14	**Trial balance**	**20,000**	**0**	**12,000**	**0**	**43,900**	**=**	**12,000**	**0**	**10,000**	**18,000**	**0**	**0**	**35,800**
IS	Depreciation		−3,000				=							−3,000
16	Cash from A/Cs Rec,			−10,700		10,700	=							0
17	Cash to A/Cs Pay.					−16,200	=				−16,200			0
18	Prepayments				2,100	−2,100	=							0
19	Salary					−16,000	=						4,000	−20,000
20	Pay PAYE					−4,000	=						−4,000	0
21	Interest received					100	=							100
22	Provision for tax						=						2,600	−2,600
23	Dividends declared						=					4,200		−4,200
24	Dividends paid					0	=					0		
25	Transfer net profit						=		6,200					−6,200
26	Balance Sheet year 1	20,000	−3,000	1,300	2,100	16,400	=	12,000	6,200	10,000	1,800	4,200	2,600	0
				36,800			=			36,800				

Andrew studied the spreadsheet again carefully. "No, it isn't like the other two is it? It is made up from the totals of all the columns, so it shows Andycabs' position at the end of the first year. I suppose it is a bit like a photograph of the company taken at a moment in time."

"Indeed it is Andrew, and the 'photographer' will be keen to take as good a picture as possible.

Just think back to the last time you took a family photo. Nine times out of ten everyone tidied themselves up, and you said, 'Smile please' just before you took the photo. They would all want to see how it had turned out, and would ask you to take it again if someone's eyes had been closed. Or think of a photograph of a football team, or the class at your old school. These are highly formalised pictures; it's a case of the tallest at the back and the smallest at the front.

It is the same with companies too; they present their 'photographs' in formal ways as well, and you can be sure that they will make them look as healthy as they can. Naturally, the Directors of a company examine their financial statements before they are published and they might well ask the Finance Director, 'Can't you improve the picture somehow, within the law, of course?'"

Classifications of assets and liabilities

The balance sheet is the oldest of the three financial statements. From our point of view, the assets part of the balance sheet tells us where a company's finances are invested, and the liabilities part tells us where those finances came from.

Noncurrent Assets

Andycabs' new car is not something that it will be selling as part of its normal trading activities; it will use it as long as it is presentable. Andrew reckoned this would be for about five years, making it a **noncurrent asset** (sometimes referred to as a **'fixed asset'**) – not a term that appealed to Andrew, "Fixed, indeed!" he exclaimed. Here again, the crucial element is time; a noncurrent asset is something that a business intends to use for longer than a year. A manufacturing company would include such things as buildings, plant and machinery, office equipment, furniture and delivery vehicles under this heading. They are all classified that way because they will not be wholly used up by the end of the current year. It's all a question of time.

Current assets

Any assets that can reasonably be expected to be converted into cash within the next twelve months are called **current assets**. Let's consider what these are, beginning with accounts receivable and cash.

Accounts Receivable and Cash

Accounts receivable are amounts owed to Andycabs by its contract customers for taxi journeys already undertaken, but which have not been paid for by its year-end. This way Andycabs 'oils the wheels', as it were.

"Will Andycabs allow these contract customers to owe it money for a year or more, though?" I asked Andrew.

"Not likely" he replied emphatically, "the business would be short of cash in no time if it had to wait that long."

It would be unreasonable to expect customers whose debts were incurred just before the end of Andycabs' current financial year to pay them before that financial year ends but they would be expected to do so within the next twelve months.

Accounts receivable, and cash itself, are also known as **liquid assets**: a term that implies a quick and easy conversion into cash, if not already being cash anyway.

Inventories

Inventories of raw materials, work–in–progress and finished products, are classified as current assets, because they are, or will become, finished products and sold within the next twelve months.

Inventories are not liquid assets; they take longer to convert into cash because they have to go through the accounts receivable stage first. (Companies that sell products for cash, like retailers, are exceptions).

Noncurrent Liabilities

Equity

Equity is made up of **Share Capital** plus **Reserves;** it is also known as **Shareholders' Funds.**

"**Reserves**, I can't help feeling it's a funny sort of term to use?" Andrew said. "I mean, I've always associated reserves with something I can draw on when I need to, like money in the bank, but here you are telling me that reserves are included in Shareholders' Funds. According to your earlier explanations, that doesn't tell me where the money is; it tells me where it came from."

Quite true, and I sympathise with Andrew's feelings concerning the use of the word, but that is how it is used in the financial world. He was quite right too, in saying that it indicates a source of funds; it is not a pot of money available for a rainy day. This is because retained profits (reserves) are accumulated from trading year after year; although they are the funds left in the business by the shareholders, they will probably have been converted into other assets – or even used to pay off liabilities. It is unlikely that they will have been held as cash. So, the equity total only tells us how much has been provided by the shareholders, either as share capital or as profits left in the business; it does not tell us where these funds have been employed.

"OK, I get the point," said Andrew, jotting down a few notes on his pad. He then checked back through some of his earlier notes, and came across the ones he'd made about provisions and suspense accounts. He noticed that 'reserves' is also the name used in America for what are called 'provisions' in the UK.

Andrew grinned "I've had this language problem before, when Joan and I were visiting friends in America. After dinner I offered to help our hostess to 'wash up' – I did not know that the right thing to offer was to 'do the dishes', no wonder she blushed, and me later, when I was told that what I had offered was to help her take a shower. You can imagine what Joan said to me afterwards!

Anyway, Richard, are there any other sorts of reserves then?"

"Yes there are. For example, if a company revalues a noncurrent asset, such as its land and buildings, it will record this by increasing the asset and by – but where do you think it will record the balancing entry?"

Andrew paused for a moment, and looked thoughtfully up at the sky. "Well, if the value of noncurrent assets goes up, then the value of the company goes up too. That means that the company's liability to its shareholders also goes up, and the only way it can record that is by increasing the value of the equity."

I was impressed. "Yes, that's right; a new column is needed, called a **revaluation reserve**, which becomes part of the equity. So, the noncurrent assets go up, and the overall shareholders' funds go up too. It's got nothing to do with operating profits, and there is no extra cash involved."

Other Noncurrent Liabilities

Long Term Debt

Loans negotiated for a period longer than twelve months, are classified as being noncurrent too. They are a significant source of funds for many businesses and frequently are for more than just one financial year.

If companies have any trade accounts payable that are not due to be paid in the next twelve months then these are classified as noncurrent liabilities, as well.

Current Liabilities

In Andycabs' case, the bank loan will be for one or two years only. If Andrew finally settles for a two–year loan, then, initially, it will be a long-term liability. When it gets to the point where it has less than twelve months left to run, it will become a **current liability**.

Current liabilities are liabilities that the company expects to pay within the next twelve months, so short term bank loans (overdrafts), trade accounts payable, Tax and PAYE (**P**ay **A**s **Y**ou **E**arn) and dividends come under this heading.

"OK, I think I've got it," said Andrew "what you're saying is that all assets and liabilities can be classified in terms of time. Noncurrent assets are assets that will be in use beyond the end of the next twelve months, and current assets are not. Similarly, noncurrent liabilities are the ones that will be outstanding at the end of the next twelve months, and current liabilities are not. How about that?"

"Very good, though there is one further distinction I want to mention. Before that, though, let's create a diagram, to illustrate what you have just said."

Figure 6.1 - The main categories of Assets and Liabilities

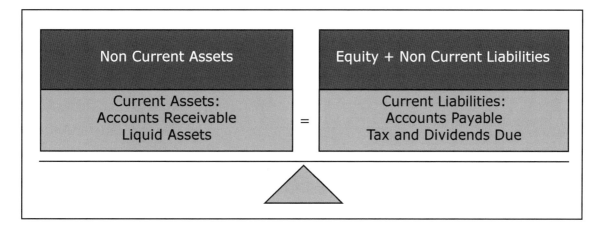

Financial Liabilities and Operating Liabilities

"Right" said Andrew, when he had studied the diagram, "I can't see any problem with that. But what's this other distinction you mentioned just now?"

"Well, there is another liabilities dimension to think about, apart from the question of time. It concerns the nature of the liability, rather than the time of its settlement."

Andrew looked puzzled. "What do you mean?"

"Think about Geoff Marsden, who owns the garage, and about Andycabs' bank. Can you think of any difference between their relationships with Andycabs?"

He thought about this for a few moments. "Well, yes" he said. "I shall be going to the bank to ask it to lend Andycabs money, and I shall be going to Geoff to buy Andycabs' fuel. Is that what you mean?"

"You're on the right track. Andycabs can use the money it borrows from the bank in any way it wants: to pay some of its suppliers' bills, for example. It is a source of money; a financial arrangement where the money is borrowed for an agreed period of time."

Andycabs' relationship with Geoff is a regular trading, or operational relationship. Although it might be argued that Geoff is lending Andycabs money while his bill is still outstanding, that is, while it is an account payable, this is not how Geoff looks at it.

"Just try asking Geoff to lend Andycabs £5,000, Andrew, when you next drive in to fill up with fuel."

Geoff will be providing the operational supplies and services needed to keep Andycabs on the road, and he will expect to be paid for them within a reasonable credit period. Bills outstanding to trade suppliers, like Geoff, are called **operating liabilities**, to distinguish them from money that has been loaned to the business under a financial arrangement. These are called **financial liabilities** and the balancing diagram needs to be revised to take this distinction into account:

Figure 6.2 - The extended Categories of assets and Liabilities - including Equity with non-current liabilities

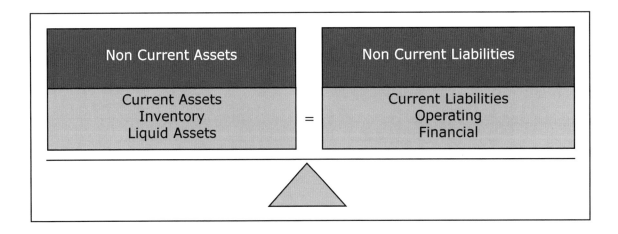

"This gives me a pretty good idea as to how I should arrange the balance sheet, so here goes," said Andrew, turning to a pad of paper.

Figure – 6.3 – Andycabs' Closing Balance Sheet Story for Year 1 – As Told By Andrew

Fixed Assets		
Car at cost	20,000	
Less depreciation	−3,000	17,000
Current Assets		
Inventory	0	
Accounts receivable	1,300	
Prepayments	2,100	
Cash	16,400	
Total Current Assets		19,000
Total Assets		36,800
Capital and Reserves		
Share capital	12,000	
Retained profit	6,200	
Shareholders' funds		18,200
Loan capital		0
Current Liabilities		
Loans and overdrafts	10,000	
Accounts payable	1,800	
Provision for tax	2,600	
Dividends due	4,200	
Total Current Liabilities		18,600
Total Liabilities		36,800

"That's very good Andrew. Your arrangement can be represented like this"

Noncurrent Assets + Current Assets = Equity + Noncurrent Liabilities + Current Liabilities
Nowadays published balance sheets are arranged as:

Noncurrent Assets + Current Assets – Current Liabilities – Noncurrent Liabilities = Equity

The left hand side of this equation is then defined as being 'net assets'. Although this definition is widely used I prefer to amend it by adding Noncurrent Liabilities to both sides, which simplifies to:

Noncurrent Assets + Current Assets – Current Liabilities = Equity +Noncurrent Liabilities

'Current Assets – Current Liabilities' is called Working Capital, and it is also known as 'Net Current Assets', thus we can write:

Noncurrent Assets + Working Capital (or Net Current Assets) = Equity + Noncurrent Liabilities

So I now have two alternative definitions which are:

Noncurrent Assets + Working Capital = Net Assets

and

Equity + Noncurrent Liabilities = Capital Employed

I prefer these definitions because they focus us on the long term assets and liabilities, not just upon equity."

Andrew was looking a bit concerned about this. "You said just now that current liabilities include bank overdrafts and other short term loans. Well, I know for a fact that many companies use bank overdrafts as if they were long-term loans; they could not repay them on demand. Yet your calculation of net assets deducts current liabilities including overdrafts. I do not think that is the correct thing to do."

Again his perceptiveness was correct.

"I agree, so what shall we do about it Andrew?"

After some thought he said "the best thing to do is to add it back to both sides, like this Net Assets + Short Term Finance = Capital Employed + Short Term Finance

I suggest we call the left hand side **Operating Net Assets**, and the right hand side **Operating Capital Employed."**

"A good idea, Andrew, let's use it from now on, and arrange Andycabs' balance sheet that way. There are now several ways that we could arrange the balance sheet so let's review them:

Firstly, we have your initial arrangement, known as a **gross balance sheet format**, because it shows the noncurrent assets and the current assets being financed by the shareholders' funds plus the noncurrent liabilities, if any, plus the current liabilities.

Secondly, we have the **net format** or **equity balance sheet format**, where both the current liabilities and the noncurrent liabilities are deducted from the assets. Most published financial reports produced in the UK use this format.

Thirdly, although I agree with the deduction of the current liabilities, I prefer to include the noncurrent liabilities as sources of finance. This gives us the **capital employed format**, or **net assets format**.

Finally, if we add back any short-term finance for instance, as you suggested Andrew, we arrive at the **operating capital employed format**, and the **operating net assets format**.

Operating capital employed is one of the most important things that you want to identify in any balance sheet."

Suddenly Andrew asked an innocent question that stopped me in my tracks. "Why is that, then?" "Why is what?" I asked.

"Well, why is operating capital employed one of the key pieces of information you would want to identify in any balance sheet? I mean, I think I know what it is, but why is it more important than working capital, or of operating net assets, for instance?"

I hadn't said that it was more important than working capital or operating net assets, but it is certainly important for two reasons, one to do with risk, and one with return.

Figure 6.4 – The Operating Capital Employed Balance Sheet

	Year 0	Year 1
Net Fixed Assets		
Car	20,000	17,000
Current Assets		
Accounts receivable	0	1,300
Prepayments	0	2,100
Cash	2,000	16,400
Total Current Assets	2,000	19,800
Current Liabilities		
Loans and overdrafts	0	10,000
Accounts payable	0	1,800
Provision for tax	0	2,600
Dividends due	0	4,200
Total Current Liabilities	0	18,600
Working Capital (Net Current Assets)	2,000	1,200
Net Assets	22,000	18,200
Add back short term loans & overdrafts	0	10,000
Operating Net Assets Financed by:	22,000	28,200
Capital and Reserves		
Capital	12,000	12,000
Retained profits (reserves)	0	6,200
Equity	12,000	18,200
Long term loans	10,000	
Capital employed	22,000	18,200
Add back short term loans & overdrafts	0	10,000
Operating capital employed	22,000	28,200

Consider risk first. If Andycabs' operating capital employed had been largely made up of long or short-term loans, then it would have to pay a lot of interest. That's fair enough, as long as the company is earning more than the interest it has to pay; it would be making good use of this loan capital. If things begin to go wrong, however, and its cash flow suffers, it may not be able to pay the interest, or repay the loans, particularly the short–term ones. Then it will be in real trouble, as will its shareholders, because they are the ones ultimately taking the risks and their shares might not be worth anything.

So the constituent parts of operating capital employed all provide valuable information, for example, the higher the proportion of loan capital, the higher the risk, especially if it is short term. A company has to pay interest on loan capital, but it doesn't have to pay dividends on its share capital if it is in financial trouble. The higher the proportion of loans, the riskier its life will be.

Now let's consider **return**.

Irrespective as to where the capital came from, a company should use it effectively. In other words, it should get the best possible 'return on its operating capital employed' that it could. 'Return' is a word that has already cropped up in phrases like 'return on investment', and 'return on capital employed'. Let's pause for a moment, and consider the difference between 'profit' and 'return'.

The income statement story (in Figure 4.2) tells us that Andycabs' forecast profit, before interest and tax, will be £13,600. This is the profit it will make from its operations and, since it is calculated before allowing for any interest that is to be received or paid, it is independent of how those operations were financed. However, this is an absolute number. It doesn't tell us anything about the efficiency of these operations. To measure that, we need to know how much profit it made on the capital invested in the business, and that's what is called its 'return'.

"So, Andrew, what sort of capital am I talking about, its equity capital, its loan capital, its capital employed, or its operating capital employed?"

Andrew could now see quite clearly where all this was leading.

"OK, you don't have to go on" he said "you mean that Andycabs' effectiveness will have to be measured in terms of how much profit it generates on its 'operating capital employed' in the business, rather than on any separate part of it?"

It didn't take him long to work out that a profit before interest and tax of £13,600 on an operating capital employed of £28,200 was equivalent to a return of about 48%. He thought that sounded great, as I did too – with some reservations that I didn't want to discuss at the time – I promised to deal with them later.

Andrew was still thinking about the two definitions of *capital employed* and of *operating capital employed* and, even though he had suggested it himself, he wanted to know exactly why it was necessary to include short-term finance.

"Well, look what happened to the bank loan on the balance sheet in Figure 6.4. It has moved from its year 0 classification as a long-term loan and it is now classified as short term finance and included in current liabilities. That's because it will become due for repayment within twelve months of the date of the balance sheet. This recognises its transitory nature, but its function will still be the same, however long or short the time period may be. It still forms part of Andycabs' financial structure, as distinct from being a trading account payable, and so it needs to be included as part of operating capital employed."

Figure 6.5 - The Operating Capital Employed Balance Sheet Building Blocks

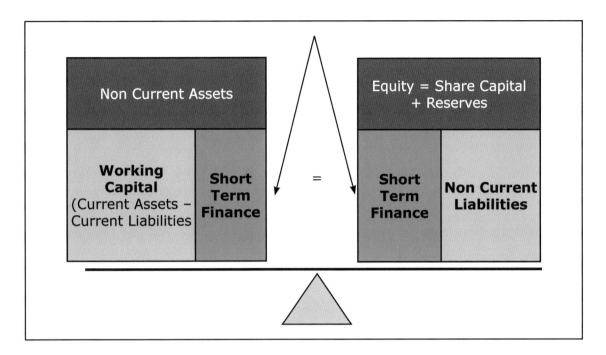

"Yes, I think I see what you mean" nodded Andrew "I'm sure I prefer the 'operating capital employed' story, too. Let me sum it up, to make sure. If all goes according to plan, Andycabs will have £17,000 of noncurrent assets at the end of year 1, and £19,800 of current assets, making a total of £36,800 in all. Most of the current assets will be funded by the current liabilities, which means that it will have a working capital of (£19,800 − £18,600 =) £1,200. Therefore, its net assets will be (£17,000 + £1,200 =) £18,200 or, looked at another way, I suppose you could also say that its equity capital of £18,200 will have been used to finance £17,000 of noncurrent assets, plus working capital of £1,200.

When I add back the short–term finance of £10,000, this gives me an operating net assets figure of (£18,200 + £10,000 =) £28,200, which, of course, equals the operating capital employed in the business, made up of the equity capital of £18,200, and the bank loan of £10,000. These are only the totals; you would need to look at the balance sheet to find the full story.

Now let me return to the income statement and cash flow stories for a moment. They tell me that Andycabs will make a net profit over the first year of £6,200 after tax and dividends paid. At this point, the equity in Andycabs will be (£12,000 + £6,200 =) £18,200. The cash position at the beginning of its trading year will be £2,000 and the cash generated from operations, after paying bank interest, will be £14,400. This means the closing cash balance will be £16,400. That can't be bad!"

He had every reason to feel satisfied, and I was very pleased that he included the income and cash flow statements in his summing–up, as well as the balance sheet. He had read them just as I had suggested he should do, like the stories in a trilogy. Each statement has its own particular story to tell, but to get the full picture he knew that he had to read them all. This was turning out to be a very worthwhile session. Andrew now felt he had a firm grasp of the information he would need once Andycabs got rolling. He had well and truly cleared the first hurdle.

"Yes, and I'm well on the way to jumping the second" Andrew assured me "because now I know where to find the information, it's all tucked away in the three main financial statements and they" he added, tapping his computer "are all tucked away in the transaction spreadsheet. So, Richard, what happens next?"

Well, judging by the time, the thing most likely to happen next was lunch. This was actually rather convenient, because I had covered all that I had wanted to – about the presentation of financial information – for the moment. It was still pleasantly warm, and Kathy brought us the menu. "Today's special is beef and mushroom pie," she told us, and we both decided to have it, accompanied by two pints of draught ale.

"It still amazes me how much we have been able to get out of that spreadsheet" Andrew said, "and the stories we have been able to tease out of the income column, the cash column, and the balance sheet rows, I wouldn't have thought it possible. But, after lunch, where do we go from here?"

"It's time to think about where Andycabs will be going from here. To do that we need to think about how its costs will change as it increases the fare miles it earns, or fails to earn, the 24,000 we have been working on so far."

Andrew looked a bit shocked. "That's true; I have been taking it for granted that it will get its 24,000 fare miles. I don't like the idea that it may not, but I can see that I ought to know what the position would be if it didn't – but how do we find out?"

"It's not difficult, Andrew" I assured him "remember that when you first showed me your estimates we talked about fixed and variable costs? Well, next time we will take another look at them, and it won't take long to see what's what."

A lot of items have been identified now; noncurrent assets, current assets, working capital, net assets, operating net assets, equity, loan capital, noncurrent liabilities, current liabilities, capital employed and operating capital employed, many of which will be useful in later chapters. In fact, the only figures that have been left out are the values of total assets and total liabilities, because we won't be using them when we analyse Andycabs' financial statements3 later on.

Summary

"Did you have a tasty lunch, Andy? I hope you were able to concentrate after it. I'm dying to hear how your day went."

"Yes, I enjoyed Kathy's beef and mushroom pie, although it wasn't as good as your steak and kidney one. It was a busy morning, I can tell you. We covered masses of things. Richard has been very helpful because he had prepared a summary of the things we were going to cover in advance. I think it will be best if you were to read this, as it will give you a better idea than if I just rely on my memory. Here it is" and Andrew handed it to her.

Joan looked at it with interest and said that she would need some time to digest it. "Make us a cup of tea, Andy, and there are some biscuits in the tin too."[3]

---

[3] In *Understand Financial Analysis, a Sherlock Holmes Approach* – a companion book, soon to be available. Check the website.

Richard's Summary

The Balance Sheet

The balance sheet shows details of a company's financial structure at a given moment in time. It is a financial snapshot of a business, showing the composition of its assets, liabilities, and equity. Companies will do all they can, within the law, to make it look as good as possible.

Two categories of **Assets** were identified; **noncurrent assets** and **current assets**, and **Liabilities** were categorised as consisting of **noncurrent liabilities,** including **equity,** and **current liabilities**.

Four balance sheet formats were identified.

The **gross version** shows total assets being balanced by total liabilities.

The **net format** balanced the equity investment with net assets, after deducting current liabilities and long-term loan liabilities.

Both of these presentations need to be amended if you want to use a **capital employed** or an **operating capital employed** approach, adding back long-term liabilities to both sides to give the first of these amendments, and in addition, adding back short-term finance gives you the second.

The term **working capital** was defined as being the difference between current assets and current liabilities; it is the extra long-term capital needed to fund the current assets that are not funded from the current liabilities. It can be negative in some companies; retail shops are an obvious example because they convert their inventories into cash very quickly. It represents the purchase of raw materials, their conversion into finished products, the sale of these products and their conversion into accounts receivable, then the settlement of these debts and so their conversion back into cash, and finally, the use of some of this cash to pay the accounts payable.

This **circulating process** is quite often called the money–go round, and, hopefully, each cycle generates more cash than it had to spend. If it does, then profit and growth will follow, but, if it doesn't, the business will eventually wither and die. The maintenance of corporate life depends on the continued circulation of cash, pumped round its system by a **healthy, profit–generating working capital heart**.

Working capital is also known as **net current assets**, a term which is quite correct, but not nearly as descriptive. It does, however, underline the essentially current nature of working capital. It embraces all the assets that will soon be converted back into cash, and all the liabilities that are due for settlement within the next twelve months.

Not all of the current liabilities are trading liabilities; some might be financial liabilities, for example, short–term loans, overdrafts, or provisions for the imminent payment of tax and dividends, etc.

Equity and Reserves

Equity is the owners' risk taking portion of the capital employed in a company. It is also known as Shareholders' Funds, and is made up of their initial investment, plus reserves. Reserves are generated by accumulating undistributed profits, or from the effects of company policy, such as the revaluation of some of the noncurrent assets of the company.

Accumulated profits retained in the business are called **Revenue Reserves**. As long as they are positive a company can pay dividends even if it has made a loss in the current year. The spreadsheet entry would be 'minus cash and minus revenue reserves'.

Capital Reserves are created as a result of policy decisions, such as the revaluation of some noncurrent asset(s), or the issue of shares at a premium price (that is, at a price which exceeds their nominal value). They are not available for distribution as dividends; they are permanently invested in the business. All reserves must be specifically labeled, to identify their origin.

Noncurrent Liabilities

Any amounts that will be owed by the company for longer than a year are classified as **noncurrent liabilities** and shown as such on the balance sheet. There are many forms, and they can be for different terms and have different interest rates.

Capital Employed and Operating Capital Employed

Capital employed refers to the sum of Equity and noncurrent liabilities. It is also equal to net assets. However, this definition is no longer as useful as it used to be, because companies are increasingly regarding short–term finance as if it were long term, thus forming part of their total funds. Therefore, the term **operating capital employed** was introduced. This needs to include all long–term and short–term capital, so short term financial liabilities must be added to the traditional long–term liabilities. The same short– term finance figure has to be added to the net assets side of the equation in order to preserve the balance, thus giving us **operating net assets**.

Andrew sat quietly, drinking his tea, whilst Joan studied this summary. She asked a few questions as she did so, and he was pleased that he could answer them effectively. At last she was finished. "You did cover a lot of ground Andy. What comes next?"

"Richard told me that we have to consider what the results will be if I achieve different fare miles to the ones we have used till now. I am looking forward to it, but it's a bit worrying too. What if I don't get as much business as I am planning for? We are meeting again at 'The Foresters' in the morning, so I shall soon know."

Joan encouraged him and told him not to worry; to her it was all sounding very positive.

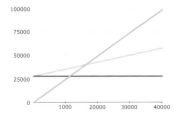

CHAPTER SEVEN

COST BEHAVIOUR AND BREAK–EVEN ANALYSIS

What will change if Andycabs achieves
more fare paying miles?

How many fare miles must it achieve
in order to cover all its costs?

These are the sort of questions that Andrew
wants to address now.

To answer them we need to return
to a topic referred to earlier -
the way costs and revenues change in relation to
levels of activity or over time.

Introduction

We were lucky, it was another lovely day, and as it was Sunday and nearly lunchtime, it seemed a good idea to see what Kathy had to offer. We could wash our meal down with a nice long, cool pint of beer and then return to my office – always quiet on a weekend – for our next session.

Andrew's appetite had obviously been whetted by our yesterday's session, because, not only did he tackle the tasty temptations of Kathy's meal with considerable relish, he kept leading the conversation back to the topic that we were going to consider this afternoon. He was very keen to get back to my office in order to check out what the effects would be if Andycabs achieved more, or less, than 24,000 fare paying miles in its first year.

"I feel much more confident now about how it all works" he said, rubbing his chin thoughtfully as, back at my office, we settled down for our afternoon session.

"Let's go back to when we first started talking about the financial statements and I'll sum up the discussion and you can tell me if I have got it right, Richard.

We started with the income statement, and the things I picked out of that were revenue, different types of costs and, finally, profit. Then we went on to the cash flow statement. Cash inflows and outflows are obviously things I shall have to keep a close eye on. When we got to the balance sheet, your main concern seemed to be to identify the different categories of liabilities and assets, so that we could see where Andycabs' money came from, and how it was being used. Then you defined operating capital employed and related Andycabs' profit before all interest and tax to it in order to see what return it was earning."

"That's fine," I agreed. "You have summed it up quite nicely. However, we should now turn our attention to the topic you kept returning to at lunch – the effect on revenues, costs, and profits if Andycabs achieves different fare miles to the 24,000 we have been using so far. Then we can look into the future and see how Andycabs is likely to develop over the years until we reach the end of the useful life of its new car. Once we have the forecasts for all five years then we can assess how well it will be doing. This is where your computer will come into its own, Andrew."

Andrew liked the idea very much, and he told me that he had already been thinking along those lines. "Obviously, as the business gets established it will have more customers, the trouble is though, I am not sure how to predict how the costs will increase, nor whether to allow for inflation in making these estimates."

"Do you think that as the costs go up with inflation, Andycabs will be able to pass on these increases to its customers by increasing fares?"

"Well" came the reply "I am fairly sure that I could pass on the increases, but I have to be competitive with other taxi firms in the town, so I would like to have the flexibility to change things in that area."

"Alright, let's build inflation into your forecasts. Then we can change your assumptions later on, if need be."

"Good, so what range of miles do you think we should consider? I've worked out that the maximum I could physically drive in a year is about 36,000 fare paying miles."

It was a fair point. "Let's calculate the costs from 0 to 40,000 fare miles in 10,000 fare mile steps," I suggested.

Fixed and variable cost behaviour

I started to remind him of our very first discussions about his forecast business expenses. Before I could be more specific, he said, "Yes. I remember, now. This was when we were talking about Andycabs' fuel and maintenance costs and you said that these were variable costs, because they will vary with the number of miles actually travelled. The road tax, insurance, licence fees and loan interest charges and my salary, on the other hand, will be fixed, or period, expenses because they will stay the same however many miles I travel."

"Fine, so we can think of the income statement in terms of those figures which will vary with miles and those which will stay fixed or at least fixed over a certain range. This means we can rewrite the income statement story in order to highlight these aspects. This is known as a marginal costing approach (known as 'direct costing in America) and it looks like this" I went over to the flip chart and wrote up the results given in figure 7.0.

Figure 7.0 – Fixed and Variable Costs and Contribution

Driven miles	48,000
Fare miles	24,000
	£
Revenue	60,000
Variable costs	
Fuel	–10,000
Maintenance etc.	–8,000
Total variable costs	–18,000
Contribution	42,000
Fixed costs	
Salary	–20,000
Depreciation	–3,000
Tax, insurance	–2,000
Telephone	–2,400
Advertising	–1,000
Total fixed costs	–28,400
Profit before financing items and tax	13,600

Andrew examined this rearrangement with interest. "You have moved things around, my salary, and the road tax and insurance are now grouped with the items that we called overheads, not with the direct expenses as we had them before. By the way, what do you mean by **contribution**?"

"Yes, I have reclassified things. They are now grouped according to their variability in relation to fare miles travelled. For that purpose, we can regard your salary as fixed, although it could also be called a **managed cost** because you decide its amount; once decided it is regarded as a fixed cost. The same is true for advertising costs too.

The concept of **contribution** is a very useful one, Andrew. It is the difference between the variable sales revenue and the variable costs. In Andycabs' case we have, for 24,000 fare miles, revenue of £60,000 and variable costs of £18,000, which gives us a contribution of £42,000.

We can look at it on a unit fare mile basis too. If we divide these figures by the 24,000 fare miles we get a fare of £2.5 and a variable cost of £0.75, giving us a contribution of £1.75 per fare mile."

"Why is that important then?" asked Andrew, who was following all this very carefully.

"Well, we know the fixed costs total £28,400, and we now know that every fare mile contributes £1.75 towards this total, so we can work out how many fare miles Andycabs has to earn in order to break–even, that is, to make no profit or loss at all. Look, £28,400/1.75 equals, approximately, 16,200 fare miles, which, when multiplied by the average income per fare mile of £2.5, gives a revenue, approximately £40,500."

I see," said Andrew thoughtfully. "Andycabs has to achieve that revenue if it is to be able to pay my desired salary of £20,000 and cover all the other fixed costs. Yes, that is a very useful concept indeed."

"If we build up a table over the range of miles I suggested, we can draw a **break–even chart**. I have filled in the first two columns, you finish the rest Andrew."

Andrew nodded, and said he was quite happy with this approach. He was keen to see the chart, as well.

Andrew made short work of this. He reasoned that all he had to do was to multiply the unit fare mile variable fuel and maintenance costs by the different ranges of miles and then deduct the fixed costs. He produced the table shown in Figure 7.1.

Figure 7.1 – The Contribution Table

Miles driven		0	20,000	40,000	60,000	80,000
Fare miles			10,000	20,000	30,000	40,000
Revenue		0	25,000	50,000	75,000	100,000
Variable costs						
Fuel		0	4,200	8,400	12,600	16,800
Maintenance		0	3,300	6,600	9,900	13,200
Total variable exists		0	7,500	15,000	22,500	30,000
Contribution		0	17,500	35,000	52,500	70,000
Fixed costs						
Salary		20,000	20,000	20,000	20,000	20,000
Depreciation		3,000	3,000	3,000	3,000	3,000
Tax, insurance		2,000	2,000	2,000	2,000	2,000
Telephone		2,400	2,400	2,400	2,400	2,400
Advertising		1,000	1,000	1,000	1,000	1,000
Total fixed costs		28,400	28,400	28,400	28,400	28,400
Profit before financing items and tax		−28,400	−10,900	6,600	24,100	41,600
Revenue		0	25,000	50,000	75,000	100,000
Variable costs		0	7,500	15,000	22,500	30,000
Fixed costs		28,400	28,400	28,400	28,400	28,400
Total costs		28,400	35,900	43,400	50,900	58,400
Fare miles		0	10,000	20,000	30,000	40,000
Contribution		0	17,500	35,000	52,500	70,000
Fixed costs		28,400	28,400	28,400	28,400	28,400

Now we can draw the break–even chart. You can see it in Figure 7.2. By the way, in America they call this chart a **profit-graph** – one might say we, in the UK, are happy if we break–even, while, in America, they want to make a profit!

Figure 7.2 The Break Even Chart

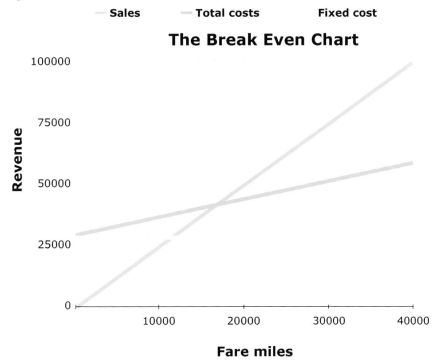

Another way of presenting this chart is just to plot the contribution line and the fixed costs line. Then, until the contribution line crosses the fixed cost line, Andycabs would be making losses; afterwards it would start earning profits. Like this:

Figure 7.3 The Contribution Chart

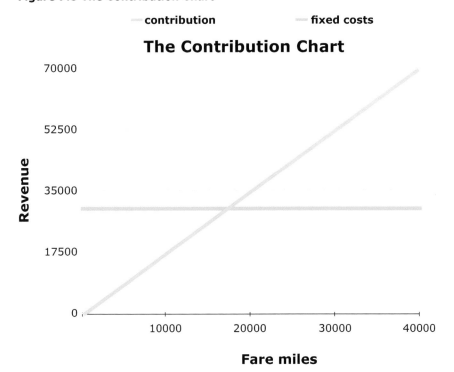

Of course the break–even point is still in the same place, things have only been rearranged to highlight the contribution line.

"Fair enough" said Andrew "it's brilliant in fact. When Andycabs has done about 16,000 fare paying miles, it will be a case of laughing all the way to the bank at £1.75 a fare mile."

"Don't forget the tax people, Andrew, they will want their share too" that cooled him down a bit.

Limitations of break–even analysis

"There are some things that worry me about this though" he said, "take the advertising cost; I don't think I could achieve 40,000 fare miles without spending more than £1,000. The same is true about the other things we have called fixed costs as well. So, surely the table is a bit wrong there?"

"Those are good points, Andrew; you decide the amount to spend on advertising in order to get extra customers. It is sometimes called an **order-getting cost**, or **managed cost**. Once you decide how much to spend it becomes a fixed cost, but one that will go up in steps as you increase that amount. Your salary is a managed cost too, because you have not related it directly to the fare miles driven. Once decided upon, it becomes a fixed cost. We can allow for these increases by adding steps to the fixed cost line."

He gazed at the contribution profile again, and said how much it had opened his eyes to the possibilities that might lie ahead. "So this is what break–even analysis is all about then," he said. "I bet a lot of businesses find this technique invaluable, don't they?"

Well, strangely enough many of them don't, because their businesses are much more complicated than that of Andycabs; the more involved they are, the more difficult it becomes to use break–even analysis. Most businesses sell a range of different products or services, each with a different rate of contribution towards the recovery of fixed costs and profit. In addition many of these fixed costs may be common to a group of products or services. In these circumstances it is impossible to work out individual break–even points. Contribution analysis is still useful to them, but individual product break–even analysis is almost certainly not[4].

"No. When it comes to the crunch," I concluded, "you probably won't be able to use break– even analysis yourself for very long, if things go well with Andycabs."

"Why on earth not?" Andrew asked, in surprise.

"Well, remember telling me that, physically, you couldn't drive more than 36,000 fare miles in a year? What will you, as company director, tell Andycabs to do if demand exceeds that number?"

"Buy another car and hire a driver" came the answer like a shot.

"Right and what would happen to its cost profile then?"

"Well, I suppose its costs would go up, but its revenues would too."

"Which costs would increase?" I persisted.

"Wait a minute," he muttered. He could guess what was coming, and wanted to prepare his ground. "It would have to get another licence, and the depreciation costs would double. The fuel and maintenance costs etc. will also go up, with the miles travelled."

"Yes, they will, and you will have to decide how the driver of the second car should be paid; a fixed salary, or a commission on the fare miles he/she travelled. In addition, a central phone operator will be needed to assign jobs between drivers. These changes mean that you will have to modify your business model and also Andycabs will now have common costs covering its two services – fare miles earned by driver 1 and by driver 2.

---

4 Dealt with in more detail in Understand Management Accounting! A companion book shortly to be available; check the website

Can you think of any other limitations that the break–even analysis may have?"

Off–hand, he wasn't sure that he could, so I prompted him to think back to our discussion concerning all the financial statements.

He looked thoughtfully at the chart again and nodded his head. "I think I can see what you're getting at, this chart is all about contribution, isn't it? It doesn't reflect cash movements or any other asset or liability movements, for that matter. It doesn't tell us anything about opening and closing balances, either, nor does it include interest received, or paid, or tax. It only tells us how different levels of activity will affect revenues and directly identifiable costs, and so profit, nothing more."

"That's right," I agreed. "Profit is obviously one of the important slices of the financial cake, but it certainly isn't the only one. Any variation in activity is going to affect many other things, apart from profit, so we ought to check those out, too."

"How do we do that, then?"

"By using this cost behaviour approach to build a financial model of Andycabs' business," I replied "but I want to leave that to our next session."

Summary

"Hello, Andy, how did you get on? Was I right - that there is nothing to worry about?"

"Well, I'm not sure, the first year looks alright, but we are going to see how things are likely to develop over the next five years next time we meet. In fact, I intend to have a go at this myself, as we won't be meeting until next Saturday. I reckon you can help me too. Look, as before, Richard has given me a summary, I'll make some tea while you read it."

Richard's Summary

Cost behaviour

Costs (expenses) can be classified according to the way they behave in relation to either time or levels of activity. Costs that do not vary with changes in the level of activity are called **fixed costs**, or **period costs**. Those that vary directly in proportion to levels of activity are called **variable costs**. In America, they are also known as **direct costs**, which, unfortunately, conflicts with the UK definition of this term, where it means directly traceable product costs, including any directly associated fixed costs.

Some costs are made up of both fixed and variable elements. Electricity is an example, because it has a fixed period charge and a variable unit one.

A straight, upwards sloping line usually represents the sum of the fixed and variable costs, that is, the total costs. This is an oversimplification because some fixed costs are only fixed for a limited range of activity. The depreciation charge is a good example, as it increases when we buy a new machine and then is constant until we buy another one. This means that the fixed cost line will have steps in it, as will the total costs line. Even the revenue line is unlikely to be a straight line, because prices may need to be altered in order to achieve higher sales volumes, giving rise to a curve instead of a straight line.

Some costs do not depend on the activity level at all. Indeed selling and advertising costs should be thought of as being the **independent variables, which** create the level of activity that is achieved. Such costs are called **managed costs**, because their level is based on management decisions as to how much to spend.

In the long run, most costs change, so specifying the time period we are dealing with is important.

Break–even analysis

Break–even analysis relates the way costs and revenues change as the level of activity changes, for a specified range of activity. The activity level at which the sales revenue is exactly equal to the total costs is called the break–even point. If the sales price is kept constant then sales revenue can be used as a measure of activity.

This information can be presented as a break–even chart or profit graph, as it is known in America. Fixed costs are usually shown as a level straight line, with the total costs, including the variable costs, being an upward sloping line located above them. (Figure 7.2)

Break–even analysis is useful in simple business situations, such as that of Andycabs, but it does have severe practical limitations. In a mixed–product situation, like a manufacturing or retail business for example, total costs only vary directly with activity if a constant product sales mix is maintained. If the product-mix changes with changes in the level of activity, then a simple break–even chart is not applicable, and this is highly likely to be the case for many businesses. Knowledge of the cost behaviour of the different products or services is still very useful for planning and control purposes; it just means that the diagram itself cannot be drawn.

The other significant limitation of this analysis is that it is only shows the effects that variations in activity levels will have on profit. All other implications, such as the effects on cash flow, or on operating net assets, are not shown.

Contribution

The difference between the selling price of a unit and its variable cost is called its contribution, that is, the amount each unit contributes towards covering the fixed costs. Only when the fixed costs have been fully recovered will subsequent units start to contribute towards profit. It can be represented in graphical form. (Figure 7.3)

As before, Joan had lots of questions and Andrew resorted to sketching diagrams in order to answer many of them. Still, he found it good to go over the day's events in this way.

CHAPTER EIGHT

MODELLING THE FUTURE

Andrew really comes into his own in this chapter.

He has prepared a model of Andycabs' business
and looked forward over the five years
that he has chosen as his planning horizon,
producing financial trilogies
for all of those years.

Introduction

The Five Year Forecasts

I arrived early in my office on Saturday morning, as I wanted to prepare the ground for what I expected to be an intensive session. Andrew joined me soon afterwards, carrying his briefcase and his laptop and looking very pleased with himself. Apparently he had been extremely busy since I last saw him.

He told me that, after our last meeting, he had decided to work out for himself how to use the spreadsheets to forecast Andycabs' operations for the next five years.

"Given our work on cost behaviour, I knew how to link these numbers to revenues and to costs, but I wasn't sure how to link the years together at first. Then I saw the light; the closing balance sheet of one year is the opening balance sheet of the next. So I got out my computer and set to work. Let me show you the printouts."

I was very impressed, and rather taken aback. The topics I had lined up to talk to him about today suddenly seemed to be obsolete.

I had better start at the beginning. First of all, I took a more critical look at the things we had identified as Andycabs' start-up information, and I decided that I had been a bit too conservative in some of those estimates and perhaps too optimistic in others. Also, I felt that I needed a better way of estimating how my fare miles might change year on year. Instead of increasing the fare miles by 10,000 a year, I decided to base it on how many days and hours I would work in the first year, and then to estimate how they would change each year. I decided that, as the number of days built up each year, I would work fewer hours per day, not by much, but it allows for any extra idle time between clients that might happen. My revised start up information is in figure 8.0:

Figure 8.0 – Andrew's Financial Forecasts

Share capital invested	£12,000
Bank loan	£10,000
Tax rate	20.00%
Pay As You Earn %	20.00%
Percentage of profit after tax to be paid as dividend	40.00%
Interest paid rate	7.00%
Interest received rate	1.25%
Cash balance held, on average	50.00%

Next I listed all the things we had identified with the car:

Figure 8.1 Andrew's car related forecasts

Car purchase	£18,000
Car fitting and initial costs	£2,000
Disposal proceeds of car	£5,000
Life of car	5 years
Total fare miles	26,400
% credit fare miles to total fare miles	20%
% miles driven to miles paid	200%
Average fare per mile	£2.25
Average fare miles per client	6
Fuel price per litre	£1.50
Miles per litre	8.20
Maintenance etc. costs per mile	£0.17

Then I estimated the running costs and how these costs would change each year.

Figure 8.2 – Andrew's business running costs forecasts

Tax, insurance etc.	£2,000
Advertising	£1,000
Telephone	£2,400
Salary	£20,000
Prepayment of tax, insurance for the next year	£2,100
Business running costs – annual increments	
Tax, insurance etc.	5%
Advertising	10%
Telephone	10%
Fare per mile percentage increase	3%
Fuel and maintenance cost increase percentage	5%
Increase in days worked per annum	15
Decrease in hours per day	0.5
Accounts receivable days	35
Accounts payable days	40

My biggest problem was how to work out the closing balances for the accounts receivable and accounts payable. I needed some way of linking these to my credit sales and to my credit purchases. Obviously this was going to be based on time. So, I thought about how many days I would be prepared to give my contract customers in which to pay, and for how long Geoff would be prepared to wait for his money. I decided that I would give my contract customers, on average, thirty–five days and that I would pay Geoff in forty days." He stopped and looked a bit embarrassed. "Well, I thought it prudent not to pay my suppliers as fast as my contract customers pay me; I'll alter it if Geoff gets upset. The way these accounts receivable and payable days work is straightforward; you divide the credit sales revenue by 365 (the days in the year) and multiply by the days you will allow for credit, or will take from the suppliers. In year 1, I expect credit sales of £11,880, so we get closing accounts receivable of (11,880/365 * 35 =) £1,139, and for accounts payable, (18,656/365*40 =) £2,044.

Now I was in a position, using my computer, to extend the spreadsheet, that we have been working on all along, for five years; however, there are two important differences that I cannot emphasise enough."

"Really, Andrew, what are they?"

"Well, until now we have been rounding up all my estimates, which made it easier for me to see how the spreadsheet was developing. Now that I wanted to extend the forecasts to a five year horizon, I realised that my more detailed forecasting methods would mean that the figures in my spreadsheet for year 1 would be different to those we had been using so far – but my new ones are better. Even so, because I am still rounding my results to whole numbers it looks as if there are tiny addition errors at times – but there are not; they are caused by the rounding."

I had to agree with him. It was better to revise the original figures so that his model would be consistent from year 1 to year 5 and to avoid using decimal places, which would only detract from the clarity of the documents.

Andrew continued "All the start-up information is in the top left hand corner above the spreadsheet. The spreadsheets we had prepared for the break–even analysis showed me how to produce the information I needed on the costs" and he produced another schedule setting them out, under yearly headings this time.

Figure 8.3 Andrew's five-year forecasts

Year	1	2	3	4	5
Fare miles	26,400	27,090	27,600	27,930	28,080
Sales revenue	59,400	62,849	65,964	68,708	71,042
Advertising	1,000	1,100	1,210	1,331	1,464
Telephone	2,400	2,640	2,904	3,194	3,514
Tax, insurance for Year 1	2,000				
Prepayment of tax, insurance	2,100	2,205	2,315	2,431	2,553
Salary – see fig 8.5	20,000	21,000	22,050	23,153	24,310
Fuel costs	9,680	9,933	10,120	10,241	10,296
Maintenance etc. costs	8,976	9,211	9,384	9,496	9,547

"This table is linked to my original estimates; the figures in it are obtained from references to the data in the top left hand corner. Therefore, when I want to change anything I can do it easily."

"With this information and approach, I could now link the spreadsheets together. Look," and he spread five of them on the table. Sure enough, the closing balance sheet row of one became the opening balance sheet row of the next, just as he had said. They are reproduced on the next few pages.

The Completed Spreadsheets

Figure 8.4 – The spreadsheet for Year 1

	YEAR 1	Car	Acc, Deprn	A/Cs Rec.	Pre-pay-ments	Cash	=	Share Cap,	Ret Profit	Bank Loan	A/Cs Pay,	Divi-dend	Tax & PAYE	Income
1	Cap tal invested					12,000	=	12,000						
2	Bank loan					10,000	=			10,000				
3	Car purchase	18,000				−18,000	=							
4	Car fittings	2,000				−2,000	=							
5	Balance Sheet year 0	20,000				2,000	=	12,000		10,000				
6	Tax, insurance, etc.					−2,000	=							−2,000
7	Advertising					−1,000	=							−1,000
8	Revenue – cash					47,520	=							47,520
9	Revenue – cred t			11,880			=							11,880
10	Fuel costs						=				9,680			−9,680
11	Maintenance/Tyres						=				8,976			−8,976
12	Telephone					−2,400	=							−2,400
13	Loan interest					−700	=							−700
14	Trial balance	20,000	0	11,880	0	43,420	=	12,000	0	10,000	18,656	0	0	34,644
15	Depreciat on		−3,000				=							−3,000
16	Cash from A/Cs Rec.			−10,741		10,741	=							
17	Cash to A/Cs Pay.					−16,612	=				−16,612			
18	Prepayments				2,100	−2,100	=							
19	Salary					−16,000	=						4,000	−20,000
20	Pay PAYE					−4,000	=						−4,000	
21	Interest received					97	=							97
23	Provision far tax						=						2,348	−2,348
24	Div dends declared						=					3,757		−3,757
25	Div dends paid					0	=					0		
26	Transfer net profit						=		5,635					−5,635
27	Balance Sheet year 1	20,000	−3,000	1,139	2,100	15,546	=	12,000	5,635	10,000	2,044	3,757	2,348	0

Figure 8.5 – The spreadsheet for Year 2

	YEAR 2	Car	Acc, Deprn	A/Cs Rec,	Fre-pay-menis	Cash	=	Share Cap,	Ret Profit	Bank Loan	A/Cs Pay,	Divi-dend	Tax & PAYE	Income
1	Opening balance sheet 1	20,000	−3,000	1,139	2,100	15,546	=	12,000	5,635	10,000	2,044	3,757	2,348	0
2	Repay bank loan					−10,000	=			−10,000				
3	Advertising					−1,100	=							−1,100
4	Revenue – cash					50,279	=							50,279
5	Revenue – cred t			12,570			=							12,570
6	Fuel costs						=				9,933			−9,933
7	Maintenance/Tyres						=				9,211			−9,211
8	Telephone					−2,640	=							−2,640
9	Loan interest					0	=							0
10	Trial balance	20,000	−3,000	13,709	2,100	52,085	=	12,000	5,635	0	21,188	3,757	2,348	39,965
11	Depreciat on		−3,000				=							−3,000
12	Cash from A/Cs Rec,			−12,504		12,504	=							0
13	Cash to A/Cs Pay.					−19,090	=				−19,090			0
14	Tax, insurance etc.				−2,100		=							−2,100
15	Prepayments				2,205	−2,205	=							0
16	Salary					−16,800	=						4,200	−21,000
17	Pay PAYE					−4,200	=						−4,200	0
18	Tax pa d					−2,348	=						−2,348	0
19	Interest received					125	=							125
20	Provision for tax						=						2,798	−2,798
21	Div dends declared						=					4,477		−4,477
22	Div dends pa d					−3,757	=					−3,757		0
23	Transfer net profit						=		6,715					−6,715
24	Balance Sheet year 2	20,000	−6,000	1,205	2,205	16,313	=	12,000	12,351	0	2,098	4,47?	2,798	0

Figure 8.6 – The spreadsheet for Year 3

	YEAR 3	Car	Acc/ Depm	A/Cs Rec.	Prepay-ments	Cash	=	Share Cap,	Ret Profit	Bank Loan	A/Cs Pay,	Dividend	Tax & Paye	Income
1	Opening balance sheet	20,000	−6,000	1,205	2,205	16,313	=	12,000	12,351	0	2,098	4,477	2,798	0
2	Repay bank loan			13,193		0	=							
3	Advertising					−1,210	=							−1,210
4	Revenue – cash					52,771	=							52,771
5	Revenue – credit			13,193			=							13,193
6	Fuel costs						=				10,120			−10,120
7	Maintenance/Tyres						=				9,384			−9,384
8	Telephone					−2,904	=							−2,904
9	Loan interest					0	=							0
10	Trial balance	20,000	−6,000	14,398	2,205	64,970	=	12,000	12,351	0	21,602	4,477	2,798	42,346
11	Depreciation		−3,000				=							−3,000
12	Cash from A/Cs Rec,			−13,133		13,133	=							0
13	Cash to A/Cs Pay.					−19,465	=				−19,465			0
14	Tax, insurance etc.				−2,205		=							−2,205
15	Prepayments				2,315	−2,315	=							0
16	Salary					−17,640	=						4,410	−22,050
17	Pay PAYE					−4,410	=						−4,410	0
18	Tax pa d					−2,798	=						−2,798	0
19	Interest received					197	=							197
20	Provision for tax						=						3,058	−3,058
21	Dividends declared						=					4,892		−4,892
22	Dividends paid					−4,477	=					−4,477		0
23	Transfer net profit						=		7,338					−7,338
24	Balance Sheet year 3	20,000	−9,000	1,265	2,315	27,195	=	12,000	19,689	0	2,137	4,892	3,058	0

Figure 8.7 – The spreadsheet for Year 4

	YEAR 4	Car	Ace, Deprn	A/Cs Rec.	Prepay-ments	Cash	=	Share Cap,	Ret Profit	Bark Loan	A/Cs Pay	Divi-dend	Tax & PAYE	Income
1	Opening balance sheet	20,000	−9,000	1,265	2,315	27,195	=	12,000	19,689	0	2,137	4,692	3,058	0
2	Repay bank loan					0	=			0				
3	Advertising					−1,331	=							−1,331
4	Revenue – cash					54,966	=							54,966
5	Revenue – credit			13,742			=							13,742
6	Fuel costs						=				10,241			−10,241
7	Maintenance/Tyres						=				9,496			−9,496
8	Telephone					−3,194	=							−3,194
9	Loan interest					0	=							0
10	Trial balance	20,000	−9,000	15,007	2,315	77,636	=	12,000	19,689	0	21,875	4,892	3,053	44,445
11	Depreciation		−3,000				=							−3,000
12	Cash from A/Cs Rec,			−13,689		13,689	=							0
13	Cash to A/Cs Pay.					−19,712	=				−19,712			0
14	Tax, insurance etc.				−2,315		=							−2,315
15	Prepayments				2,431	−2,431	=							0
16	Salary					−18,522	=						4,631	−23,153
17	Pay PAYE					−4,631	=						−4,631	0
18	Tax paid					−3,058	=						−3,058	0
19	Interest received					269	=							269
20	Provis on for tax						=						3,249	−3,249
21	Dividends declared						=					5,199		−5,199
22	Dividends paid					−4,892	=					−4,892		0
23	Transfer net profit						=		7,798					−7,798
24	Balance Sheet year 4	20,000	−12,000	1,318	2,431	38,349	=	12,000	27,487	0	2,163	5,199	3,249	0

Figure 8.8 – The spreadsheet for Year 5

	YEARS	Car	Ace. Deprn	A/Cs Rec,	Pre-pay-ments	Cash	=	Share Cap	Ret Profit	Bank Loan	A/Cs Pay	Divi-dend	Tax & PAYE	Income
1	Opening balance sheet	20,000	−12,000	1,318	2,431	38,349	=	12,000	27,487	0	2,163	5,199	3,249	0
2	Repay bank loan						=							
3	Advertising					−1,464	=							−1,464
4	Revenue – cash					56,834	=							56,834
5	Revenue – credit			14,208			=							14,208
6	Fuel costs						=				10,296			−10,296
7	Maintenance/Tyres						=				9,547			−9,547
8	Telephone					−3,514	=							−3,514
9	Loan interest						=							
10	Trial balance	20,000	−12,000	15,526	2,431	90,205	=	12,000	27,487	0	22,006	5,199	3,249	46,221
11	Depreciation		−3,000				=							−3,000
12	Cash tram A/Cs Rec.			−14,164		14,164	=							
13	Cash to A/Cs Pay.					−19,832	=				−19,832			
14	Tax, insurance etc.				−2,431		=							−2,431
15	Prepayments				2,553	−2,553	=							
16	Salary					−19,448	=						4,862	−24,310
17	Pay PAYE					−4,862	=						−4,862	
18	Tax pa d					−3,249	=						−3,249	
19	Interest received					340	=							340
20	Provision for tax						=						3,364	−3,364
21	Dividends declared						=					5,382		−5,382
22	Dividends paid					−5,199	=					−5,199		
23	Transfer net profit						=		8,074					−8,074
24	Balance Sheet year 5	20,000	−15,000	1,362	2,553	49,567	=	12,000	35,561	0	2,175	5,382	3,364	0

It was a pretty impressive achievement on Andrew's part.

"So, Andrew, now that you have prepared them how are you going to use them?"

"That's no problem either. You remember how we extracted the trilogy of stories from the spreadsheet for year 1?" he paused while I agreed that I did remember. "Well, I have extracted them for the whole of the five years from these spreadsheets and written them side by side."

He produced yet three more sheets, giving the income statements for all five years, followed by the cash flows and the balance sheets. "When you have had a chance to study these I'll have a go at interpreting them for you," he said.

Figure 8.9 – Andycabs' Forecast Income Statements – variable costing format

	Year 1	Year 2	Year 3	Year 4	Year 5
Revenue Cash	47,520	50,279	52,771	54,966	56,834
Credit	11,880	12,570	13,193	13,742	14,208
	59,400	**62,849**	**65,964**	**68,708**	**71,042**
Variable Expenses					
Fuel	−9,680	−9,933	−10,120	−10,241	−10,296
Maintenance etc.	−8,976	−9,211	−9,384	−9,496	−9,547
	−18,656	**−19,144**	**−19,504**	**−19,737**	**−19,843**
Contribution	**40,744**	**43,705**	**46,460**	**48,971**	**51,199**
Fixed Expenses					
Salary	−20,000	−21,000	−22,050	−23,153	−24,310
Advertising	−1,000	−1,100	−1,210	−1,331	−1,464
Tax, Insurance and Licence Fees	−2,000	−2,100	−2,205	−2,315	−2,431
Telephone	−2,400	−2,640	−2,904	−3,194	−3,514
Depreciation	−3,000	−3,000	−3,000	−3,000	−3,000
	−28,400	**−29,840**	**−31,369**	**−32,993**	**−34,719**
Profit before all interest and tax	**12,344**	**13,865**	**15,091**	**15,978**	**16,480**
Non operating income	97	125	197	269	340
Profit before interest payable (PBIT)	**12,441**	**13,990**	**15,288**	**16,247**	**16,820**
Loan Interest	−700	0	0	0	0
Profit before tax (PBT)	**11,741**	**13,990**	**15,288**	**16,247**	**16,820**
Provision for taxation at 20%	−2,348	−2,798	−3,058	−3,249	−3,364
Profit after tax (PAT)	**9,392**	**11,192**	**12,230**	**12,998**	**13,456**
Dividends	−3757	−4,477	−4,892	−5,199	−5,382
Retained profits	**5,635**	**6,715**	**7,338**	**7,799**	**8,074**

Figure 8.10 – The Cash Flow Statements

	Year 1	Year 2	Year 3	Year 4	Year 5	Total
Operating Cash Inflows						
Revenue–Cash	47,520	50,279	52,771	54,966	56,834	262,370
Cash from accounts receivable	10,741	12,504	13,133	13,689	14,164	64,230
Total Cash Inflow from Operations	**58,261**	**62,783**	**65,904**	**68,655**	**70,998**	**326,601**
Operating Cash Outflows						
Advertising	−1,000	−1,100	−1,210	−1,331	−1,464	−6,105
Telephone	−2,400	−2,640	−2,904	−3,194	−3,514	−14,652
Tax, insurance, etc.	−2,000					−2,000
Pay to Accounts Payable	−16,612	−19,090	−19,465	−19,712	−19,832	−94,709
Prepayments (Tax, ins, etc.)	−2,100	−2,205	−2,315	−2,431	−2,553	−11,604
Salary	−16,000	−16,800	−17,640	−18,522	−19,448	−88,410
Pay tax on Salary	−4,000	−4,200	−4,410	−4,631	−4,862	−22,103
	−44,112	−46,035	−47,944	−49,821	−51,672	−239,583
Cash Generated From Operations	**14,149**	**16,747**	**17,961**	**18,835**	**19,325**	**87,017**
Financial Cash Inflow (Interest Received)	97	125	197	269	340	1,027
Gross Cash From Operations	**14,246**	**16,872**	**18,157**	**19,103**	**19,666**	**88,044**
Financial charges						
Dividends paid	0	−3,757	−4,477	−4,892	−5,199	-18,325
Tax paid	0	−2,348	−2,798	−3,058	−3,249	−11,453
Bank interest paid	−700	0	0	0	0	−700
Total financial charges	−700	−6,105	−7,275	−7,950	−8,448	−30,477
Cash available for Long Term Investment	**13,546**	**10,767**	**10,882**	**11,154**	**11,218**	**57,567**
Long Term Investments						
Car purchase	−18,000	**0**	**0**	**0**	**0**	−18,000
Car fittings	−2,000	**0**	**0**	**0**	**0**	−2,000
Total long term investments	−20,000	0	0	0	0	−20,000
Cash Available for Financial Use	−6,454	10,767	10,882	11,154	11,218	37,567
Financial Sources						
Loans repaid	0	−10,000	0	0	0	−10,000
Shares issued	12,000	0	0	0	0	12,000
Bank loan	10,000	0	0	0	0	10,000
	22,000	−10,000	0	0	0	12,000
Change in Cash Held	**15,546**	**767**	**10,882**	**11,154**	**11,218**	**49,567**

Figure 8.11 Balance sheets for the years ending 31st March

	Year 0	Year 1	Year 2	Year 3	Year 4	Year 5
Non Current Assets						
Car	20,000	17,000	14,000	11,000	8,000	5,000
Current Assets						
Accounts receivable	0	1,139	1,205	1,265	1,318	1,362
Prepayments	0	2,100	2,205	2,315	2,431	2,553
Cash	2,000	15,546	16,313	27,195	36,349	49,567
Total Current Assets	2,000	18,785	19,723	30,776	42,098	53,482
Current Liabilities						
Loans and overdrafts	0	10,000	0	0	0	0
Accounts payable	0	2,044	2,098	2,137	2,163	2,175
Provision for tax	0	2,348	2,798	3,058	3,249	3,364
Dividends due	0	3,757	4,477	4,892	5,199	5,382
Total Current Liabilities	0	18,150	9,373	10,087	10,611	10,921
Working Capital (net current assets)	2,000	635	10,351	20,689	31,487	42,561
Net Assets	22,000	17,635	24,351	31,689	39,487	47,561
Add back short term loans & overdrafts	0	10,000	0	0	0	0
Operating Net Assets	22,000	27,635	24,351	31,689	39,487	47,561
Financed By:						
Non Current Liabilities						
Capital	12,000	12,000	12,000	12,000	12,000	12,000
Retained profits (reserves)	0	5,635	12,351	19,689	27,487	35,561
Equity	12,000	17,635	24,351	31.689	39,487	47,561
Long term loans	10,000	0	0	0	0	0
Capital Employed	22,000	17,635	24,351	31,689	39,487	47,561
Add back short term loans & overdrafts	0	10,000	0	0	0	0
Operating Capital Employed	22,000	27,635	24,351	31,689	39,487	47,561

The Income Implications

"Let's start with the income story, as you can see" he said "the revenue, fuel and maintenance costs all increase in line with the fare mile increases and with their forecast price increases. I have built in an annual increase for the fixed costs too. Interest earned was a bit tricky, and I used the method you described to me of totaling the cash column just before calculating it, and assuming that 50% of that total would be earning interest for the year. Profits increase every year, even though my salary is increasing every year too." Andrew was looking very pleased with himself.

Next he turned to the cash flow statements.

The Cash Flow Implications

"Except for the first year when the car and fittings will be bought, Andycabs will generate sufficient cash from its operations each year to cover its outgoings and build up an increasing cash balance. It will be able to repay the bank loan at the beginning of year 2, thus saving a year's interest charge. Just look at that total of cash over the five years. I always felt sure Andycabs would do well, but if it achieves this it will be beyond my dreams.

The Balance Sheet Implications

I can see from these balance sheets that the car is going to be down to a book value of only

£5,000 by the fifth year, as expected, of course, for this was my estimate of its disposal value. It will need replacing, but there will be plenty of cash available. The loan will have been paid off, and life looks good."

There was no doubt about it, Andrew had done a very good job indeed, and I told him so. The way he had extracted the information from the spreadsheets and drawn up the financial trilogy told me that he really was mastering the subject.

Andrew has discovered the power of his computer; he is now able to alter his estimates and see what difference this would make to the results. This is often referred to as carrying out a **what if** analysis. For example, what if the average fare per mile in year one would be £2.00 rather than his planned one of £2.25? What if Andycabs' relationship between fare miles and miles driven is different to the one initially planned?

It is now possible to discover which variables Andrew should concentrate on in order to maximise Andycabs' profits. All one has to do to answer such questions as these, is to change the relevant item(s) in the original figures that are in the top left hand corner, above the year 1 spreadsheet. The model looks something like this:

Figure 8.12 - The Modeling Process

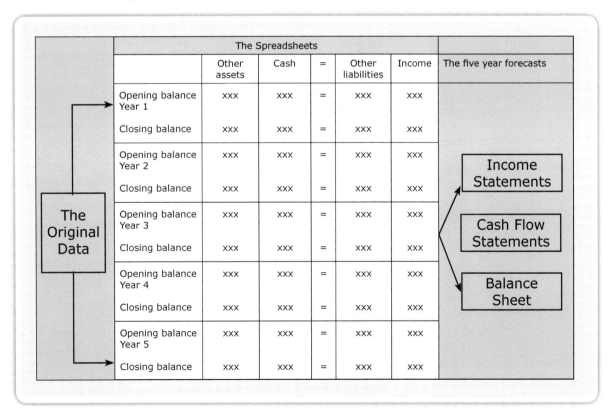

Andrew was feeling very cheerful and suggested that we should stroll down to 'The Foresters' where he would buy a round of drinks to celebrate. It was almost lunchtime so I had no objection to that idea.

When we had arrived, and while Andrew was fetching our drinks, I decided to carry straight on with a new topic, because he was obviously on top of things now.

It was time to talk about the key ratios that would help him to assess the state of Andycabs' activities. At the same time I wanted to broaden the discussion so that he could use these ideas when he eventually got round to investing some money in companies other than Andycabs. I told him as much when he arrived back at our table.

"Hmm" he murmured "you must be impressed with these numbers if you are thinking about my becoming an investor in the shares of other companies already. I do like the idea though, in fact, it was one of my original hopes," he added with his mischievous grin.

Richard's Summary

Andrew has used his computer to produce five years of forecasts of Andycabs' operations. From these he extracted the trilogy of financial statements and interpreted them too. He was very pleased with the results.

Now he is able to alter his estimates and see what difference this would make to the results. This is often referred to as carrying out a 'what if' analysis.

It had been a good morning, and I knew that Andrew was keen to continue after lunch.

CHAPTER NINE

A MATTER OF INTERPRETATION

Having the forecast figures for all five years, means that
there are very many numbers to assess.

Using ratios simplifies the task, but they often raise
more questions than they answer.

Then it's time to sharpen up your detective skills.

Introduction

Having finished our lunch and after the waitress had cleared our table, we got down to business again.

"You took me by surprise this morning, Andrew, but it was a very nice surprise, because you have produced all the material I needed for me to address the next topic, which is how you can use ratios to help you keep an eye on Andycabs' performance and also uncover potential ways to increase it. I call it '**revealing the secret money hidden in your business**'. However, let's go back to basics for a moment.

When we were discussing the various ways of presenting the data in the balance sheet, we identified several definitions for capital employed and for net assets. We eventually decided that the operating capital employed format was the best one for us to use when we were going to work out ratios. Well we are at that point now, so let's reproduce figure 6.5 as figure 9.0, and refresh our minds as to why it is important."

Figure 9.0 - The Balance Sheet Relationships (=)

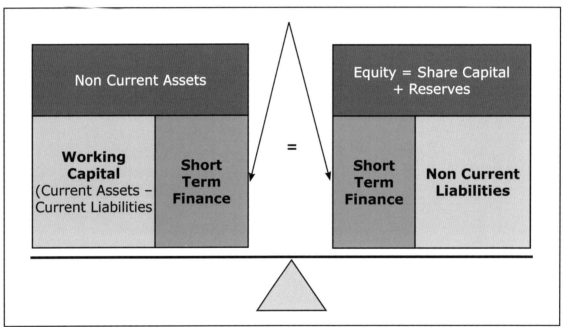

Andrew studied it with interest. "It makes the relationships much clearer. For example, it is easy to see that the relationship between equity and loans is important. I wouldn't like the proportion of loans to operating capital employed to get too big for the reasons you discussed before, when you were talking about risk. I can see that the relationship between current assets and current liabilities is important too, I wouldn't like it to go negative."

Earlier on in our discussions the topics of risk and return had come up several times. These are important areas for Andycabs and ratios can indicate how well it is doing. Let's start with the question – **is it financially healthy**?

Solvency, Liquidity and Risk

I asked Andrew to suggest a couple of variables which, when expressed as a ratio, would give us some indication of financial risk.

"Oh, I don't think there's much doubt about that" he said, "this must be what you had in mind when you were talking about the operating capital employed balance sheet. It's all to do with the way in which operating capital employed is split between equity and loan capital, both short and long term, isn't it? They must be the variables we need and, since we have been talking a lot about risk increasing as the amount of loans increase, I would express this relationship as"

Long and Short term Loans
Operating Capital Employed

Once again, he was on target. We can also see from the balance sheet diagram that this could also be expressed as:

Long and Short Term Loans
Equity + Noncurrent liabilities + Short Term Loans

It is called the **Debt Ratio** and is expressed as a percentage.

"Hang on a minute, though" said Andrew. "You have included short term finance in operating capital employed, do all analysts do that?"

"Well, no, they don't. There are several other definitions that they use, and I will discuss these with you when you feel ready to invest in other peoples companies. But let's reproduce the relevant reports here before we do any calculations.

Figure 9.1 – The Balance Sheets for years 0 and 1

	Year 0	Year 1
Non Current Assets		
Car	20,000	17,000
Current Assets		
Accounts receivable	0	1,139
Prepayments	0	2,100
Cash	2,000	15,546
Total Current Assets	2,000	18,785
Current Liabilities		
Loans and overdrafts	0	10,000
Accounts payable	0	2,044
Provision for tax	0	2,348
Dividends due	0	3,757
Total Current Liabilities	0	18,150
Working Capital (net current assets)	2,000	635
Net Assets	22,000	17,635
Add back short term loans & overdrafts	0	10,000
Operating Net Assets	22,000	27,635
Financed By:		
Non Current Liabilities		
Capital	12,000	12,000
Retained profits (reserves)	0	5,635
Equity	12,000	17,635
Long term loans	10,000	0
Capital Employed	22,000	17,635
Add back short term loans & overdrafts	0	10,000
Operating Capital Employed	22,000	27,635

Figure 9.2 – The published format for the income statements

	Year 1	Year 2	Year 3	Year 4	Year 5
Revenue	47,520	50,279	52,771	54,966	56,834
	11,880	12,570	13,193	13,742	14,208
	59,400	**62,849**	**65,964**	**68,708**	**71,042**
Direct Expenses:					
Salary	20,000	−21,000	−22,050	−23,153	−24,310
Tax, insurance and licence fees	−2,000	−2,100	−2,205	−2,315	−2,431
Fuel	−9,680	−9,933	−10,120	−10,241	−10,296
Maintenance	−8,976	−9,211	−9,384	−9,496	−9,547
	−40,656	−42,244	−43,759	−45,205	−46,584
Gross Operating Profit	18,744	20,605	22,205	23,503	24,458
Overhead Expenses					
Advertising	−1,000	−1,100	−1,210	−1,331	−1,464
Telephone	−2,400	−2,640	−2,904	−3,194	−3,514
Depreciation	−3,000	−3,000	−3,000	−3,000	−3,000
	−6,400	−6,740	−7,114	−7,525	**−7,978**
Profit before all interest	**12,344**	**13,865**	**15,091**	**15,977**	**16,480**
Non–operating income	97	125	197	269	340
Profit before interest payable (PBIT)	**12,441**	**13,990**	**15,288**	**16,246**	**16,820**
Loan interest	−700	0	0	0	0
Profit before tax (PBT)	**11,741**	**13,990**	**15,298**	**16,246**	**16,820**
Provision for taxation @ 20%	−2,348	−2,798	−3,058	−3,249	−3,364
Profit after tax (PAT)	**9,392**	**11,192**	**12,230**	**12,997**	**13,456**
Dividends	−3,757	−4,477	−4,892	−5,199	−5,382
Retained profits	**5,635**	**6,715**	**7,338**	**7,798**	**8,074**

Here are his results for the first year.

Debt Ratio

Andrew was soon busy with his computer again. "Hmm, let's see, the higher the debt ratio the riskier the business. The definition is 'all loans divided by operating capital employed' 10,000/27,635 – equals about 36%. That looks reasonable to me." I agreed, but pointed out that, to be sure, he should calculate another ratio that is also a measure of the level of risk. This is called **Interest cover**, and it shows how many times the available profits would cover the interest payments. "Good idea, let's see, I need to include interest received as it's also available to pay the interest due" he said and calculated the following:

Interest Cover

PBIT/Interest payable; 12,441/700, about 18 times. "My goodness" he exclaimed "that must be safe."

The debt and interest cover ratios measure the extent of Andycabs exposure to the risk of being unable to service its interest payments or to repay its loans.

Current Ratio

While on the subject of risk, there are two other ratios to consider, which focus on Andycabs' ability to meet its short-term trade debts as they fall due.

"Which variables would you select to help us with this?" I asked.

"Let's see" he said. "I think you are referring to Andycabs' current liabilities, because that's why they are called current."

"Fine" I agreed "and where will it get the money from to pay them?"

Andrew paused, and then said "I see, it has to collect it from its accounts receivable if there is not enough in the bank."

"Yes, and, if it had any, even its inventories could be converted, first to accounts receivable and then to cash, in fact, all of its current assets are available for conversion into cash in order to settle its current liabilities."

"Ah, that's the other variable, then," he exclaimed, "we have to relate current assets with current liabilities."

That was correct. It is called the **current ratio** and is calculated simply by dividing the current assets by the current liabilities.

Andrew looked at the balance sheet, (figure 8.11 reproduced as figure 9.1 above) and turned to his computer again. "I see" he said. "So, at the end of the first year, we expect the current assets to be £18,785, and the current liabilities to be £18,150. That gives us a current ratio of about 1. Is that right?"

It is. It means that Andycabs would have as many current assets as it would need to settle all its current liabilities, if called upon to do so. This includes the ability to pay off the bank loan, which is now classified as a current liability because it will be repayable within a year.

Andrew wanted to know what sort of risk this represented, and the answer is hardly any, since Andycabs' forecast cash balance would be enough on its own to pay the trade accounts payable, the taxes and to repay the loan.

"Why did you leave out dividends in what you just said" asked Andrew "and does this mean that we want the current ratio to be as big as possible then, in order to be safe?"

"I left out the dividend figure because this is under the control of the directors and ultimately the shareholders. Concerning your second point, no, not really, because a high ratio may indicate that a company has too much of its capital tied up in inventory or accounts receivable, or even as plain old cash. You have to keep those assets working."

"But surely" Andrew persisted "the smaller the ratio, the higher the risk of Andycabs being unable to settle its short term debts? Does this mean that a current ratio of less than one is high–risk?"

"Not necessarily. Some companies can survive quite satisfactorily with a current ratio of less than one. Their ability to do so depends on how quickly they can convert their inventory and accounts receivable into cash. If this happens quickly, as it does with many retailers for example, then although the total owing in accounts payable may exceed the current assets, they will still be paid regularly and frequently, hence the suppliers will be happy with the situation."

Although we have been considering just the ratios for one year, it is better to work them out for several years and to look at trends. The time to worry is when the figures start sliding down a slippery slope.

Acid Test or Quick Ratio

"There is another ratio in this family that provides an even harsher measure of liquidity. This is the **acid test**, or **quick ratio**, which measures the number of times Andycabs' current liabilities are covered by its liquid assets, rather than its current assets."

Andrew looked thoughtful for a moment. "Let's see" he said. "Liquid assets is the name for accounts receivable and cash, and any other items that can be quickly turned into cash isn't it?"

"Yes, that's right" I replied. "Inventories are left out because, generally, they take longer to turn into cash."

"Not if you are a retail shop like Marks & Spencer or Walmart; they turn their inventories into cash quicker than Andycabs can collect its accounts receivable."

Andrew was quite correct. Companies belong to different categories, or types. For example, the heavy industry category is hardly likely to have the same values for its ratios as the retail shop category; hence one has to be careful when comparing one company with another. Another example would be Andycabs itself, which has no inventories. In its case the acid test ratio will be the same as the current ratio.

And, yes, Andrew did make a joke about 'The Forester's' products being the best liquid assets he knew!

Performance Ratios

Now it was time to think about measuring performance, and Andrew was very pleased with that idea.

Return on Operating Net Assets

"And I can anticipate the first comment you are going to make" he said, you are going to suggest we see how well Andycabs has been using its operating net assets to create profits." He was right again.

"But which profit figure shall we use Andrew?"

"We have already discussed this and I remember that it is the profit before all interest and tax" he replied. "Because that will tell me how much profit it has made from its trading operations" and he was back to his computer in no time.

Return on Operating Net Assets (%)

Profit Before all Interest and Tax/Operating Net Assets; 12,344/27,635, about 45%. "We can do a bit more detective work here, Andrew, because this ratio can be thought of as being the prime ratio at the top of a pyramid of ratios. Let's take a look at it."

Figure 9.8 - The Key Ratio Pyramid

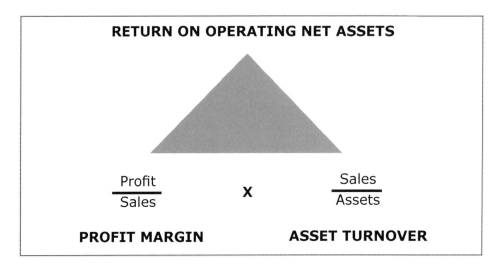

"Hey! This is just like those exercises we used to do in mathematics classes at school, you know, something like this" and Andrew wrote out the expression below:

$$\frac{1}{5} \times \frac{5}{6} = ?$$

"This one equals 1/6 because you cancel the common factors. I always wondered if anyone ever used it."

"Ah, but financial people love it, and use it all the time" I replied. "Let's begin by looking at the profit margin first."

Profit Margin, or Profitability

The profit margin measures the operating efficiency of a business by calculating how much profit it generates from its sales revenue.

Andrew was ready with his computer again. "Fair enough" he said. "I am quite happy with that. This means that, with total sales revenue of £59,400, and a profit, before all interest and tax, of £12,344, its profit margin during the first year will be 12,344/59,400, about 21%."

Andrew had a thoughtful expression on his face as he turned back to the income statement, in Figure 9.2.

"There's just one thing that bothers me about this, though" he said, "if you hadn't prompted me into picking out the profit before all interest and tax, I might have suggested that the profit margin should be based on the **gross operating profit** of £18,744. Surely, that's one of the first things a lot of business people would check out?"

This was a fair question. The ratio he had in mind is the **gross margin**, or **gross profit margin**, as it is also called, rather than the profit margin. It measures the amount of profit generated from sales revenue after deducting only those costs that are directly associated with the production of the products, or the provision of services sold.

In Andycabs' case, this would be the figure that Andrew mentioned, namely, the gross operating profit of £18,744. In a shop, it would be equivalent to the sales revenue of the goods sold, less the cost of those goods. In a manufacturing company, the **cost of goods sold** would also include the manufacturing costs directly associated with the production of the goods, some of which may be allocated fixed costs[5].

The profit margin, on the other hand, is based on the profit remaining after the deduction of all (direct and indirect) operating expenses. Both ratios are useful. Some analysts use profit before interest paid in this calculation, thus including interest received as part of operational profits. If used consistently it gives similar results.

"But, Richard, what if we were to use the variable costing format shown in figure 8.9? There the contribution margin is shown as £40,744, because only fuel and maintenance etc. costs have been deducted from sales revenue. This gives a result of 69%?" "That's true, Andrew, and it is also a useful figure, but it is not one that is available in the published financial statements of companies; hence, I am not using it here. We did discuss its importance to you earlier."

Asset Turnover or Activity.

This ratio is also a measure of performance. It tells one how many times the assets have been turned over in terms of sales revenue in a year. The more times, the better, as it means the assets are working harder. Asset turnover equals sales/operating net assets and Andrew had This worked out in no time: 59,400/ 27,635, about 2.1 times.

---

5 This topic is dealt with in "Understand Management Accounting", check the website.

"Look Andrew, let's multiply these two ratio results together; 21 % x 2.1, about 45% – as it should.

Andycabs is obtaining about a 45% **return on operating capital employed** by having a profit margin of around 21% and turning its assets over about 2.1 times. This can be improved by increasing the profit margin, or by reducing the operating net assets, or by increasing sales revenue for the same level of assets."

Andrew was looking very thoughtful, and I guessed he was thinking about my earlier comment concerning *knowing his numbers and so unlocking the hidden profits in his business.*

Return on Equity

"Now let's assess the return that you and Joan can look forward to from your own equity stakes in the business" I suggested.

This is the sort of question that can be relied upon to strike a responsive chord with Andrew and I asked him to select the two variables that would give us a ratio to provide us with this information.

He didn't have much trouble with this, either. "Well, it's got to be based on the figure for our equity capital, hasn't it? And we're talking about return, which brings in one of the profit figures. There isn't any doubt about the choice here either; because we have already agreed that profit after tax is the part the shareholders can call their own. You described it as the point where Andycabs says, 'OK folks, this is where I get off'."

Turning to his computer again, he said "OK, let's have a look at the figures; we've got to relate a profit after tax of £9,392 to the (end of year) equity stake of £17,635. That gives me a return of about 53%; very much better than I could get if I left my money in the building society."

But then he paused. "That's all very well for a large company, but in Andycabs' case it's a bit risky to draw that conclusion. In the first place both the **return on equity** and the **return on operating capital employed** are going to be appreciably affected by the salary I get paid. If my salary is small these returns would be big and vice versa."

He was right, of course, and he also had to think of the money he could have earned working for somebody else and letting their capital work for them in a bank or building society. The **opportunity cost** as we described it earlier. Still, if he is consistent in the salary that Andycabs pays him, these ratios will provide a useful indicator of performance over time.

Dividend cover

Like interest cover, this ratio tells us how many times a particular level of profit covers an external commitment. This time, we are looking at the profit after tax, to see how many times it covers the dividends that have been declared. It also indicates the directors' philosophy concerning paying out money to the shareholders as compared to reinvesting it in the company's own activities, such as its future expansion.

For Andycabs we have: $\dfrac{\text{Profit after tax}}{\text{Dividend}} = \dfrac{9,392}{3,757} = 2.5 \text{ times}$.

Not surprising really, as Andrew had already decided to take out 40% as dividend in his model.

"OK. I'm getting the message" he said. "Are you sure that there aren't any more ratios I should use, while we're at it?"

We have probably examined as many ratios as Andrew will need for his taxi business, but, as said before, this is a comparatively uncomplicated scenario. Business analysts and financial managers in larger companies will need to calculate more ratios than suggested here. These other ratios are important, but they are not appropriate for Andycabs' operations.[6]

The Five Year View

Now that Andrew had calculated the ratios for the first year he was keen to look at the story they would tell for all five years of operations that he had forecast, as shown in figure 9.4.

Figure 9.4 – Measuring Andycabs' performance

Operating Performance	Year 1	Year 2	Year 3	Year 4	Year 5
ROCE (= RONA) [Operating}	45%	57%	48%	40%	35%
Profit Margin (%)	21%	22%	23%	23%	23%
Net Operating Assets Turnover	2,1	2.6	2.1	1.7	1.5
Gross Profit Margin (%)	32%	33%	34%	34%	34%
Working Capital Performance	**Year 1**	**Year 2**	**Year 3**	**Year 4**	**Year 5**
A/Cs Receivable Days	35	35	35	35	35
A/Cs Payable Days	40	40	40	40	40

Figure 9.5 – Risk and shareholder performance

Risk and Liquidity	Year 1	Year 2	Year 3	Year 4	Year 5
Debt Ratio (Including Short Term)	36%	0%	0%	0%	0%
Interest Cover (Times)	18	N/A	N/A	N/A	N/A
Current Ratio	1.0	2,1	3.1	4,0	4.9
Shareholder Performance	**Year 1**	**Year 2**	**Year 3**	**Year 4**	**Year 5**
Return On Equity	53%	46%	39%	33%	28%
Dividend Cover [Times]	2.5	2.5	2,5	2,5	2.5

We have used a new grouping of the ratios, which makes good sense. The first group gives us information on how well Andrew will be managing the business. The second group tells him if the business will be in a risky position and the third group shows him how well Andycabs will be performing for its shareholders.

"Let's graph these ratios over time, to get an idea of their trends" I suggested. But Andrew was examining the trends of the profit margin and the gross margin. "Look at those figures, I knew I was making the right decision to go into business by forming Andycabs - as long as it gets results as good as I have forecast, that is."

Indeed they do look good, but let's examine the graphs before commenting on them individually.

---

6 They will be discussed in detail in Understand Financial Statements, a Sherlock Holmes Approach – a companion book to this one

Andycabs Performance Graphs

Figure 9.6 - Return on Net Operating Assets Chart

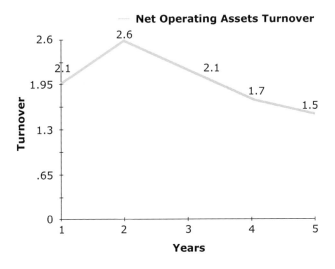

Figure 9.7 - Net Operating Assets Turnover Chart

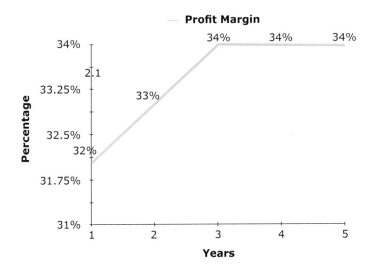

Figure 9.8 - Profit Margin Chart

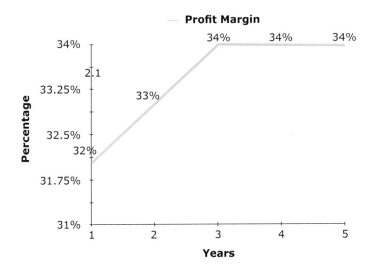

Andycabs will have a return on its operating capital employed which peaks at about 57%. That pleased Andrew, but he wondered why it was trending downwards from then on.

"To answer that let's look at its constituent ratios, the profit margin and the asset turnover. As you can see, the profit margin at first trends upwards and then remains constant, whilst the asset turnover, after the second year, is trending downwards." Andrew was following my words with great attention.

"We see that the operating net assets are budgeted to increase by over 100% in five years, whilst sales revenue is only budgeted increase by 20%. The asset turnover trend is strongly influenced by this growth in assets year on year, particularly of cash, which will increase from £2,000 to over £49,000. Hence the asset turnover is bound to fall. Since the fall in asset turnover is greater than the increase in profit margin, the return on operating net assets is bound to fall too."

"How can I increase the profit margin then?" asked Andrew.

"Well, to improve the profit margin you need to examine each cost in turn to see if you can make any savings in them and you should also consider whether you could increase your charges per mile. Again, it's a case of unlocking the hidden profits in your business."

How well is Andycabs serving its shareholders?

"Here we need to look at the trend of the return on equity ratio."

Figure 9.9 - Return on Equity Chart

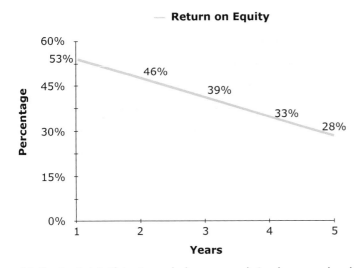

At first sight this trend depressed Andrew, who had expected to see it growing over time.

"Let's see what this trend would look like if I didn't take any salary at all" he said, turning to his computer. He found that, although the return on equity went up, it still trended downwards. Why is that then?"

"Although you have improved the profit after tax by not taking a salary, Andycabs is still building up cash, and so the equity is increasing too. How can you put that right Andrew?"

The answer came pretty quickly. "I can increase the dividend rate and take the cash out" he said. Back to the computer, up went the dividend rate to 100% and the return on equity reached over 100% by year 5.

"What does this suggest to you Andrew?"

He was looking puzzled. "It's very odd, if I choose a 100% dividend rate the return on equity improves dramatically. If I leave the money in the business Andycabs seems to make a mess of things."

"That is actually what is happening. Andycabs is only getting 1.25% on the money it has in the bank, and only on half that amount, because that is the way you set up the model when you built it. Its overall performance is being diluted by the poor return it is getting on a major part of its assets. What does that suggest to you, Andrew?"

"Well, it's pretty obvious really. If Andycabs can get a better return in the taxi business than it can get by leaving the money in the bank, as I see that it can, then it should use the cash to expand the business, buy another taxi (or two), hire some drivers and make even more money."

"Yes, that is what I meant when I described cash as being a facilitating asset; income is only created when it is turned into profitable trading assets and a bank deposit at such a low rate of interest is hardly that."

I wasn't sure he was listening though; he was thinking about the new fleet, I could see it in his eyes.

I had to bring him back to earth. "How much more money will you be making if you do expand the business?"

Andrew paused. "I know what you mean; I'll have to amend my model and work through how the costs and revenues will change if extra cars and drivers are added. Fair enough, but I'm not going to get into that now."

It was time to move on and consider how risky Andycabs' business might be.

The Risk Profile of Andycabs

As we have seen, if all goes well Andycabs will be paying off the bank loan just after the end of its first trading year. With no debt thereafter it has no financial risk, although its trading risks still remain. Still, for the sake of completeness, let's have a look at the graph of the debt ratio.

Figure 9.10 - The Debt Ratio Chart

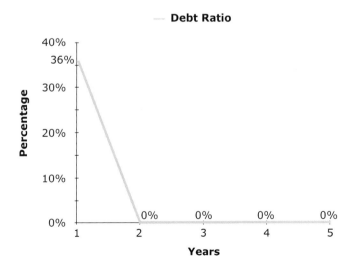

As you can see, it looks very safe indeed: safe enough for Andrew to consider whether Andycabs ought to borrow more money from the bank in a year or two, when it has established a track record.

"Borrow more money?" Andrew was surprised.

"Why not? If Andycabs can earn a better return than the interest rate that it has to pay to the bank, then the extra will increase the return the shareholders get."

This is where the debt and interest cover ratios come into their own. They can be used as planning tools to balance the added returns with the added risk. You can have too little, as well as too much, loan capital in your business. It's another example of how knowing your numbers enables you to unlock the hidden money in your business.

Andrew was not convinced. He felt that if Andycabs expanded too quickly, it would run into all sorts of problems, and this could be true. Many companies make this mistake.

Now let's look at short–term risk. Do the current assets exceed the current liabilities? By how much?

The Current Ratio

The strong upward trend is due to the retention of cash in the business. It is not necessarily a good sign. In Andycabs' case we have seen that the cash is being used in a rather unprofitable way. Although part of working capital, it is not working hard enough. I would prefer to see Andrew planning better business uses for it, converting it into better profit earning assets.

Figure 9.11 The Current Ratio Chart

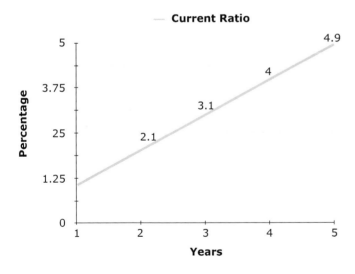

For the sake of completeness we should look at accounts receivable and accounts payable days, but since Andrew had decided what these were to be when building his model, they won't be informative to us here. When Andycabs is really trading, they will be important, because if a company's **accounts receivable days** are increasing whilst its **accounts payable days** are not, then it could be heading for cash flow trouble. Not a problem for Andycabs, if Andrew's forecasts turn out to be correct.

Figure 9.12 - Working Capital Days Chart

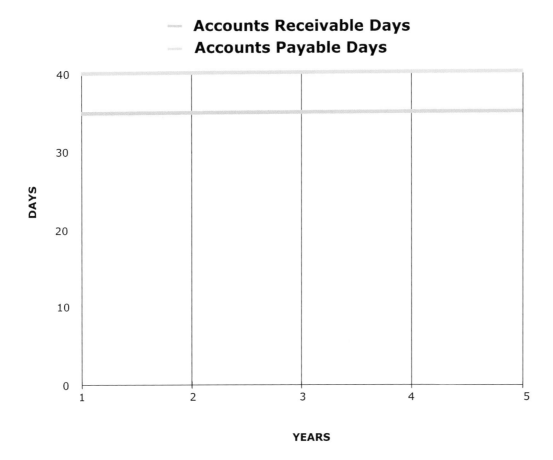

The Cash Flow Statement

So far in this meeting we have concentrated on ratios, but another important source of information, if not the most important one that must not be neglected, is the cash flow statement. A company can be unprofitable for a time and still survive, but if it loses cash in significant amounts it is likely to cease trading. Cash is like blood, if you lose enough of it, or if it stops circulating then.... but what a depressing thought. Andycabs' cash flow looks very healthy- **see Figure 9.13**.

Figure 9.13 – Operating cash flows (summarised)

	Year 1	Year 2	Year 3	Year 4	Years 5	Totals
Operating cash inflows						
Revenue –cash	47,520	50,279	52,771	54,966	56,834	262,370
Cash from accounts receivable	10,741	12,504	13,133	13,689	14,164	64,230
Total cash inflow from operations	**58,261**	**62,783**	**65,904**	**68,655**	**70,998**	**326,601**
Operating cash outflows						
Advertising	−1,000	−1,100	−1,210	−1,331	−1,464	−6,105
Telephone	−2,400	−2,640	−2,904	−3,194	−3,514	−14,652
Tax, insurance etc.	−2,000					−2,000
Pay to accounts payable	−16,612	−19,090	−19,465	−19,712	−19,832	−94,709
Prepayments (tax, ins, etc.)	−2,100	−2,205	−2,315	−2,431	−2,553	−11,604
Salary	−16,000	−16,800	−17,640	−18,522	−19,448	−88,410
Pay tax on salary	−4,000	−4,200	−4,410	−4,631	−4,862	−22,103
Total cash outflow from operations	**−44,112**	**−46,035**	**−47,944**	**−49,821**	**−51,672**	**−239,583**
Cash generated from operations	**14,149**	**16,747**	**17,961**	**18,835**	**19,325**	**87,017**
Financial cash inflow (interest received)	97	125	197	269	340	1,027
Gross cash from operations	**14,246**	**16,872**	**18,157**	**19,103**	**19,666**	**88,044**
Financial charges						
Dividends paid	0	−3,757	−4,477	−4,892	−5,199	−18,325
Tax paid	0	−2,348	−2,798	−3,058	−3,249	−11,453
Bank interest paid	−700	0	0	0	0	−700
Total financial charges	**−700**	**−6.105**	**−7.275**	**−7.950**	**−8,448**	**−30,477**
Cash available for long term investment	**13,546**	**10,767**	**10,882**	**11,154**	**11,218**	**57,567**
Long term investments						
Car purchase	−18,000	0	0	0	0	−18,000
Car fittings	−2,000	0	0	0	0	−2,000
Total long term investments	**−20,000**	**0**	**0**	**0**	**0**	**−20,000**
Cash available for financial use	**−6,454**	**10,767**	**10,882**	**11,154**	**11,218**	**37,567**
Financial sources						
Loans repaid	0	−10,000	0	0	0	−10,000
Shares issued	12,000	0	0	0	0	12,000
Bank loan	10,000	0	0	0	0	10,000
	22,000	**−10,000**	**0**	**0**	**0**	**12,000**
Change in cash held	**15,546**	**767**	**10,882**	**11,154**	**11,218**	**49,567**

Cash generated from operations is expected to grow healthily each year, and will be supplemented with interest earned. From year 3 onwards there will be cash available for Andycabs to invest in expanding its business or to invest in other ways. The company looks as if it will be cash positive; all in all, a very good-looking situation.

Time for Andrew to spread his wings

"Now, Andrew, I know that you are interested in investing in other companies one day and, as I have often told you, their profiles will be different according to which industry they belong, so I have put several of them on my website, www.understandaccounting.com, and you can work your way through them; they all have answers, of course."

"That's interesting, what sorts of businesses are there?"

"Well, there is a public house – Kathy let me use 'The Foresters'; there is a shoe shop; a bookshop; Geoff's garage; a manufacturer; and I am planning to add many more."

"Well, I shall have a look at them and have a go too; I am glad you have included answers though!"

"So there it is, Andrew, I have now completed my story about the language of business and introduced you to modeling and to financial analysis and suggested how you can take this further on your own. However, it's now up to Andycabs to prove itself, and I will follow its progress with a great deal of interest."

Andrew looked a little smug. "I've not been sitting on my hands all this time, you know. I went to see the bank manager with my projected financial statements – you were right, by the way, she gave me a thorough going over, and was particularly concerned about my revenue forecasts and cash flows – still, I opened Andycabs' bank account, got the loan, and - but come with me to the car park for a minute."

I did as I was asked, and there, was Andycabs' new car, resplendent with roof sign and with a bold **ANDYCABS** painted on the door.

"Care to come for a spin? No charge this time." What could I say?

After our trip I suggested to Andrew that we should have one final meeting, because he had expressed an interest in the origins of the language of business on several occasions. He readily agreed and he asked me if Joan could come too as she wanted to know how the spreadsheet tied in with the traditional **double entry system** of **debits** and **credits** that she was used to and which is used by all companies in all countries in the world. Of course I agreed and indeed, having heard so much about her from Andrew I was looking forward to meeting her.

Summary

"My, you have had a long session today Andy."

"You're telling me! It was very interesting though and there is a lot to tell. In fact, as before, it would be best if you were to read Richard's own summary while I get dinner ready for a change. By the way, we are going to cover how the spreadsheet links in to double entry next time. Would you like to come too, as I know you are very interested in it?"

"That's great, I'll look forward to it; I'm free most afternoons." Andrew handed her the summary and went off to the kitchen to see if he could find anything that he could cook.

Richard's Summary

Ratios are useful when assessing; a company's operating performance, its performance on behalf of its shareholders; and its risk profile.

Operating Performance

Operating performance is indicated by the **return on operating net assets (or operating capital employed)**. This can be broken down into its **profit margin** and its **asset turnover**. Companies in different industries have very different ratio results. Companies in service industries, like Andycabs, tend to have high asset turnovers, because they do not possess many assets. Those in heavy industries, on the other hand, tend to have low asset turnovers. Ratios in the retail industry would be different again. One has to be careful to compare like with like.

Financial Performance

Financial performance is measured by the **return on equity** and by the **dividend cover**. Both are somewhat suspect if it is a small business because the owners can decide whether to have higher salaries and lower dividends, or vice versa. No doubt, they will choose the most tax effective method for them personally.

Risk

Risk is measured with the **debt ratio**, and with other ratios not discussed here because they are not relevant to Andycabs' operations. **Interest cover** is also a useful measure of risk. The amount of debt a company can safely have depends upon the quality, that is to say, the predictability and steadiness, of its cash flow. Too little debt can be as bad for the shareholders as too much, because their company may be missing opportunities to earn profits at a rate that exceeds the loan rate of interest it would have to pay.

The current ratio, acid test, inventory days, accounts receivable days and accounts payable days all help us to assess short term risk. Of course, in Andycabs' case there are no inventory days – a stock of customers to be drawn upon at will would be nice! – but where and how would one keep them?

Trends

Ratios tell much more interesting stories when there are several year's worth; even so, they often raise more questions than they answer. It is better not to use too many decimal places because the underlying financial numbers aren't that accurate. Graphs are useful.

Cash Flow

In the final analysis a good company generates cash and a bad one loses it. Trends of cash sources and uses are very illuminating. A company that cannot generate sufficient cash from its operations to fund its expansion over a long period may be getting into trouble. The more it has to borrow, the higher the interest it has to pay. Often companies in these positions have to ask their shareholders for extra money to bail them out: not a thing the shareholders like very much.

The cash flow format used in published accounts is difficult to interpret (probably because an easily understood statement would reveal more than the directors would be comfortable with). In **Understand Financial Statements - A Sherlock Holmes Approach** (as already noted, a companion book to this) I explain how to convert the published cash flow statement into a much more revealing document.

Finally, I suggested to Andrew that he should visit my website, which is called, www. understandaccounting.com, where he would find examples of other companies to work through, with answers, of course.

"Dinners up" called Andrew. "I chickened out and we have oven chips and microwave cod fillets."

"Good old fish and chips – I might have guessed it" answered Joan with a laugh. "That summary was very interesting. There are some things I want to talk to you about though, after we have eaten."

CHAPTER TEN

A LITTLE BIT OF HISTORY – CRACKING THE PACIOLI CODE!

In 1494 a now famous monk, Luca Pacioli, wrote a book that captured all that was known about mathematics at that time.

In an appendix to it he described the double entry system that is still used by every company in all the world today.

Unfortunately for us, he did not record the logical approach that he must have employed; instead he laid down a set of rules;

rules which are still being taught without any understanding as to why they work.

Now, for the first time in 500 years, the logic that underlies the system is revealed in this chapter.

Introduction

It was about two weeks since I had seen Andrew, who had been busy getting the Andycabs' business under way. I had heard about it, of course, through my own clients, most of whom spoke very favourably about the friendly and efficient service he was giving, so I was very pleased when he made an appointment to come round for our final meeting.

He arrived, with his wife, just as coffee and biscuits had been put on the table in my conference room.

"I've been looking forward to this" he said, with his cheeky grin. "You make the best cup of coffee in the neighbourhood."

After introducing me to Joan and then bringing me up to date with his activities, he told me he was very glad I had suggested today's meeting. "I have been hearing a lot about debits and credits lately, and I haven't a clue what they are" he told me. He was also keen to hear about how the whole system got started in the first place. Joan added that she too was very interested "I know how debits and credits work, but not why they work as they do."

"We have to go back a long way into the mists of time" I replied "the first major evidence of its development was in an appendix to a book written in 1494, by a Franciscan monk who was also a mathematician, Luca Pacioli, in Venice". [*Pacioli had important friends, one of whom was Leonardo da Vinci; you can see Pacioli visiting him in the picture at the beginning of this chapter*]

Pacioli was only nineteen when he was invited to go to Venice at the invitation of a merchant, who wanted him to teach commercial arithmetic, and accounting methods, to his three sons. Naturally Pacioli had to learn how accounts were being kept before he could teach them, and the merchant helped him by involving him in his own business activities. Pacioli learned the bookkeeping rules, by rote, as we still do today. However, when he came to write his book, many years later, I am certain that he would have made sure that there was a logical foundation to the bookkeeping system. His thinking would have developed like this:

He would have started with the same equation that was used throughout this book, that is

'Assets = Liabilities'

Then he would have concluded that the system recognised a business as being a person in its own right, separate from its owners, so the merchant's capital was also a liability from its point of view.

His next step would have been to introduce profit, as we did earlier, giving him:

Assets = Liabilities + Profit

Next he would have replaced profit with 'Revenue–Expenses' to give:

Assets = Liabilities + Revenue – Expenses

Then he would have eliminated the 'minus expenses' from the right hand side by adding it to both sides to give:

Assets + Expenses = Liabilities + Revenue

This explained why assets and expenses were dealt with in the same way in the accounting system he was investigating; similarly for liabilities and revenues.

Finally, to make the system self balancing he would have eliminated the right hand headings by subtracting them from both sides, leaving him with:

$$\text{Assets} + \text{Expenses} - \text{Liabilities} - \text{Revenues} = 0$$

As this was self-balancing, always equaling zero, he was able to ignore the equals sign and the zero altogether!

"I remember this" said Andrew "will you show how some of Andycabs' earlier transactions would be dealt with please?"

"Certainly, Andrew, here is a list of some of them."

Figure 10.0 Some of Andycabs Original Entries

Capital invested	12,000
Bank loan	10,000
Revenue – cash	48,000
A/cs Rec	12,000
Salary	20,000
Tax on salary	4,000

The first entry would be

Cash	Share Capital	
12,000	−12,000	= 0

Then we get

	Cash	Share Capital	Bank loan	
	12,000	−12,000		= 0
	10,000		−10,000	= 0

The cash revenue items would be entered as:

Cash	Share Capital	Bank Loan	Revenue	
12,000	−12,000			= 0
10,000		−10,000		= 0
48,000			−48,000	= 0

Credit revenue items would involve creating an accounts receivable column and the entry would be of the type:

A/CS Rec.	Revenue	
12,000	−12,000	= 0

Notice that every entry now has a positive item balanced by a negative one, totaling zero.

To record Andrew's salary new columns would be needed too, with entries of this type:

Cash	Salary	PAYE	
−16,000	20,000	−4,000	= 0

Although we now have three entries on a line, they still total to zero. The original spreadsheet would now look like this:

Figure 10.1 – The amended spreadsheet (in £'000)

	YEAR 1	Car	Ace. Deprn	A/Cs Res.	Prepay-ments	Cash	Share Cap,	Ret Profit	Bank Loan	A/Cs Pay.	Dividend	Tax & PAYE	Income
1	Capital invested					12,000	−12,000						0
2	Bank bar					10,000			−10,000				0
3	Car purchase	18,000				−18,000							0
4	Car fittings	2,000				−2,000							0
5	Balance Sheet year 0	20,000	0	0	0	2,000	−12,000	0	−10,000	0	0	0	0
6	Tax, insurance, etc.,					−2,000							2,000
7	Advertising					−1,000							1,000
6	Revenue – cash					48,000							−48,000
9	Revenue – credit			12.000		0							−12,000
10	Fuel costs					0				−10,000			10,000
11	Maintenance/Tyres					0				−8,000			8,000
12	Telephone					−2,400							2,400
13	Loan interest					−700							700
14	Trial balance	20,000	0	12,000	0	43,900	−12,000	0	−10,000	−18,000	0	0	−35,900
15	Depreciation		−3,000			0							3,000
16	Cash from A/Cs Rec			−10,700		10,700							0
17	Cash to A/Cs Pay					−16,200				16,200			0
18	Prepayments				2,100	−2,100							0
19	Salary					−16,000						−4,000	20,000
20	Pay PAYE					−4,000						4,000	0
21	Interest received					100							−100
23	Provision for tax					0						−2,600	2,600
24	Dividends declared					0					−4,200		4,200
25	Dividends paid					0					0		
26	Transfer net profit					0		−6,200					6,200
27	Balance Sheet year 1	20,000	−3,000	1,300	2,100	16,400	−12,000	−6,200	−10,000	−1,800	−4,200	−2,600	0
						36,800						−36,800	

111

"Remember, Andrew, this is the simple version of the spreadsheet. I talked earlier about the expanded spreadsheet, with columns for every expense and revenue item and explained that these were temporary accounts that would be transferred to the income column, which itself would be transferred to retained profits. The expanded approach could be applied here too, but, as I told you before, it would only complicate my explanations, because its spreadsheet would not fit onto one page!

Now let's consider the next aspect that Pacioli examined. He noted that each column contained both plus and minus figures, making it difficult to see how much came in and how much went out of these columns. He saw too that the double entry method he was documenting had two columns under each heading, one for plus items and one for minus ones, so he replicated this in his original equation:

$$\text{assets}^+ + \text{assets}^- + \text{expenses}^+ + \text{expenses}^- = \text{liabilities}^+ + \text{liabilities}^- + \text{revenues}^+ + \text{revenues}^-$$

Let's put some transactions in to illustrate:

+	assets$^+$	+	assets$^-$	+	expenses$^+$	+	expenses$^-$	=	liabilities$^+$	+	liabilities$^-$	+	revenues$^+$	+	revenues$^-$
Invest capital	12,000							=	12,000						
Pay expenses			3,000		3,000										
Cash revenues	5,000							=					5,000		

As before, he wanted to eliminate the right hand entries by amending **both** sides of the equation. The liabilities side will look like this:

liabilities$^+$	+	liabilities$^-$	+	revenues$^+$	+	revenues$^-$	+	liabilities$^+$	+	liabilities$^-$	+	revenues$^+$	+	revenues$^-$
12,000										12,000			
				5,000									5,000

This right hand side equals zero because the items under the plus and minus headings cancel each other out. Notice, too, that all the signs between the headings are plus ones, so they can be left out.

The complete expression now looks like:

assets$^+$	assets$^-$	expenses$^+$	expenses$^-$	liabilities$^+$	liabilities$^-$	revenues$^+$	revenues$^-$
12,000					12,000		
	3,000	3,000					
5,000							5,000

The equation has disappeared and so have any signs attaching to the numbers in the system, because they are implied by the columns that they are in. We can see that every left hand entry is balanced with a right hand one.

Pacioli knew that there was no way in which the clerks would have understood his algebraic explanation, and he realised that was why the left hand and right hand entries had been given names. This led him back to his religious training, because he knew that, in Latin, the verb **Debere** referred to an obligation, accountability, or charge, and **Credere** referred to trust, belief, faith. Thus, when a company receives things for which it has to account, it has an obligation, so the amount is entered as a **debit**. The person who hands over these things to the company trusts it, has faith in it, so his account is **credited**. So now all the clerks had to learn was that **debits** go on the left of an account and **credits** go on the right.

The instruction Debit (**DR**) means 'enter an amount on the left hand side of an account' and the instruction Credit (**CR**) means 'enter an amount on the right hand side of an account'. There is no connotation of good or bad about them; they are just location instructions. Thus the double entry system is based on the rules of algebra;

112

it is not a 'set of conventions', as it has been regarded as being for hundreds of years; rules that had to be learned by rote and applied by rote too!

The spreadsheet would now look like this:

Figure 10.2 - The spreadsheet with sub-columns (in £'000)

	Car		Ace. Depm		A/Cs rec.		Prepay-ments		Cash		Share Cap.		Ret Profit		Bank		A/Cs Pay.		Dividend		Tax & Paye		Income	
	Dr	Cr	Dr	Cr	Dr	Cr	Dr	Cr	Dr	Cr	Dr	Cr	Dr	Cr	Dr	Cr	Dr	Cr	Dr	Cr	Dr	Cr	Dr	Cr
Cap tal Invested									12.0			12.0												
Bank Loan									10.0							10.0								
Car Purchase	18.0									18.0														
F ttings Purchase	2.0									2.0														
Tax, Ins. Etc.										2.0													2.0	
Advertising										1.0													1.0	
Revenue - Cash									48.0															48.0
Revenue - Credit					12.0																			12.0
Fuel Costs																		10.0					10.0	
Maintenance/Tyres																		8.0					8.0	
Telephone										2.4													2.4	
Loan Interest										0.7													0.7	
Depreciation				3.0																			3.0	
Cash From A/Cs rec.						10.7			10.7															
Cash To A/Cs Pay.										16.2							16.2							
Prepayments							2.1			2.1													20.0	
Salary										16.0												4.0	20.0	
Pay Paye										4.0											4.0			
Interest Received									0.1															0.1
Trial Balance	20.0	0.0	0.0	3.0	12.0	10.7	2.1	0.0	80.8	64.4	0.0	12.0	0.0	0.0	0.0	10.0	16.2	18.0	0.0	0.0	4.0	4.0	47.1	60.1
Provision For Tax																						2.6	2.6	
Dividends Declared																				4.2			4.2	
Dividends Pa d																								
Transfer Net Profit														6.2									6.2	
Balances	20.0	0.0	0.0	3.0	12.0	10.7	2.1	0.0	80.8	64.4	0.0	12.0	0.0	6.2	0.0	10.0	16.2	18.0	0.0	4.2	4.0	6.6	60.1	60.1

Each account has two columns with a line down the centre to separate them. Nowadays these are called 'T' accounts

"But the balances have been lost! How does the system deal with that?" asked Andrew.

"That was no problem; remember that minus signs are taboo in the system – much too likely to lead to arithmetical errors – so both columns are added up and made equal by increasing the smaller side and writing the same sum on the opposite side under a ruling off of the account. Let's try Pacioli's method of getting the balances back, just using Andycabs cash account to illustrate."

The result is given in Figure 10.3. It works nicely. What is more, it separates the periods and clearly identifies the balance for the beginning of the next period.

Figure 10.3 – The Cash Account

YEAR 1	Cash	
	DR	CR
Capital invested	12.0	
Bank loan	10.0	
Car purchase		18.0
Car fittings		7.0
Tax, insurance, etc.		2.0
Advertising		1.0
Revenue – cash	48.0	
Revenue – credit		
Fuel costs		
Maintenance/Tyres		
Telephone		2.4
Loan interest		0.7
Depreciation		
Cash from A/Cs Rec.	10.7	
Cash to A/Cs Pay.		16.2
Prepayments		2.1
Salary		16.0
Pay PAYE		4.0
Interest received	0.1	
Trial Balance	80.8	64.4
Balancing figure		16.4
Totals	80.8	80.8
Balance brought down	16.4	

The only accounts that will have balances in them in the balance sheet are the asset and liability accounts. The income column does not have a balance to 'bring down' because its amount will have been transferred (closed) to the retained profit account.

The accumulated depreciation account has been placed in the asset section (even though it is the only account with a credit balance in that section) because it is so closely linked with the car, and it is clearer if the two are kept together. Most financial systems would group it with the liabilities section.

"My goodness, the merchants must have had very long spreadsheets then to cope with all these accounts," added Joan.

As a matter of fact they didn't; they solved the problem by, in effect, cutting up the spreadsheet into separate columns, each becoming a separate 'account'. Then they grouped them into different books, called ledgers, according to their similarity. For example all the accounts receivable would be in one ledger. This was effective, but the concept of an equation lying at the heart of the system was now obscured.

"You told me earlier that everything could be in balance but still be wrong because items could have been left out, put in twice, put in the wrong accounts or even have been got back to front! How was that guarded against?" asked Andrew.

"Pacioli saw that the merchants entered a description of every transaction into a book, called a journal, with an instruction as to how they were to be entered into the ledgers; that is, as debits and credits. This allowed the merchant, or his appointed auditors, to go back to the journal to check that the entries had been made correctly."

"So the auditors do have a function in life after all" commented Joan "I will be more tolerant of them in future. But what a pity Pacioli did not record his algebraic explanation for us – just think, for 500 years we have been learning the rules by rote without understanding why they worked at all."

And all I could do was to agree with her wholeheartedly.

The 'debit', 'credit' system of 'double entry' works, of course, but many people are confused by these terms and there are several reasons for that.

First of all, people cannot understand why assets, which are nice things to have, and expenses, which are not, are dealt with in the same way in the double entry system; they both increase with debits and decrease with credits. We know why, don't we? It's because assets and expenses are on the same side of the original equation, and, in any case, assets are only expenses waiting to happen. The difference between them is just a matter of time.

The second problem comes about because liability and revenue accounts have most of their entries on the right hand side, whilst asset and expense account ones have most of theirs on the left. Just look at the bank loan account and the car account above, for example.

People see that left hand entries (debits) **increase** both asset and expense accounts but they **decrease** liability and revenue ones. No wonder they find it confusing. The same is true for credits, which decrease asset and expense accounts and increase liability and revenue ones.

Banks don't help either. The statements they send us present the balances on them from the bank's point of view. Thus they regard us as assets if we have borrowed money; we are their accounts receivable (Debtors) and the statement shows a debit balance. If we have deposited money they regard us as liabilities because they owe us this money; we are their accounts payable (Creditors) – and the statement shows a credit balance. Naturally, given that scenario, we soon come to believe that credits are nice things to have whilst debits are not.

It's all right if you appreciate the logic that I have just explained, but for the last five hundred years this explanation has been lost. Even most financial people are unaware of why the system works in the way that it does – they know **how**, but not **why**. They learned the rules, of which the golden ones are:

'Debits go on the left of an account and credits go on the right'.

'For every debit entry there must be a credit one'.

'Debit the account that receives, and credit the account that gives'.

"That's the way I learned it." Joan said. "As I said a few minutes ago, this is the first time I have understood why it works."

"Well, that's very interesting" said Andrew "but I would like to see the spreadsheet again, with all this included, just to complete the picture, so to speak?"

"Yes, Andrew here it is again, with arrows on the first two accounts to illustrate how the balances are carried down"

Figure 10.4 - The double entry spreadsheet

Year 1	Car Dr	Car Cr	Ace. Depm Dr	Ace. Depm Cr	A/Cs Rec. Dr	A/Cs Rec. Cr	Prepayments Dr	Prepayments Cr	Cash Dr	Cash Cr	Sh Cap Dr	Sh Cap Cr	RET Profits Dr	RET Profits Cr	Bank Dr	Bank Cr	A/Cs Pay Dr	A/Cs Pay Cr	Dividend Dr	Dividend Cr	Tax & Paye Dr	Tax & Paye Cr	Income Dr	Income Cr
Capital Invested									12.0			12.0												
Bank Loan									10.0							10.0								
Car Purchase	18.0									18.0														
Car Fittings	2.0									2.0														
Tax, Insurance, Etc.,										2.0													2.0	
Advertising										1.0													1.0	
Revenue - Cash									48.0															48.0
Revenue – Credit					12.0																			12.0
Fuel Costs																		10.0					10.0	
Maintenance/ Tyres																		8.0					8.0	
Telephone										2.4													2.4	
Loan Interest										0.7													0.7	
Depreciaton				3.0																			3.0	
Cash From A/Cs rec,						10.7			10.7															
Cash To A/Cs Pay.										16.2							16.2							
Prepayments							2.1			2.1														
Salary										16.0												4.0	20.0	
Pay Paye										4.0											4.0			
Interest Received									0.1															0.1
Trial Balance	20.0	0.0	0.0	3.0	12.0	10.7	2.1	0.0	80.8	64.4	0.0	12.0	0.0	0.0	0.0	10.0	16.2	18.0	0.0	0.0	4.0	4.0	47.1	60.1
Provision For Tax																						2.6	2.6	
Div dends Declared																				42			4.2	
Div dends Paid																								
Transfer Net Profit													5.2										6.2	
Trial Balance	20.0	0.0	0.0	3.0	12.0	10.7	2.1	0.0	80.8	64.4	00	12.0	00	6.2	0.0	10.0	16.2	18.0	0.0	4.2	4.0	6.6	60.1	60.1
Bring Down Balances Totals		20.0	3.0			1.3		2.1		16.4	12.0		6.2		10.0		1.8		4.2		2.6			
	20.0	20.0																						
	20.0	20.0	3.0	3.0	12.0	12.0	2.1	2.1	80.8	80.8	12.0	12.0	6.2	6.2	10.0	10.0	18.0	18.0	4.2	4.2	6.6	6.6	60.1	60.1
Balances Brought Down	20.0			3.0	1.3		2.1		16.4			12.0		6.2		10.0		1.8		4.2		2.6		

	Debits Total	=	Credits Total
	36.8		36.8

Both Andrew and Joan were very pleased with this explanation of the double entry system. Andrew felt he could hold his head high in future discussions when the topic arose. "I'm jolly glad you did not use the double entry system before this, though, I would have had a much harder time understanding everything we have done together.

I can see how you would introduce expense and revenue columns in this final spreadsheet too, so there's no need for you to illustrate it. I can see, too, why people get into such a muddle over which side to put things on, in fact I've got a story which just illustrates the problem" and he settled back with a smile.

"A Martian landed on Earth on a cruelly cold winter's day, with lots of snow on the ground. Mars, I think, is a very warm planet, so he was desperate to find shelter. Seeing a woodsman's house he knocked on the door and was invited in. Once inside, he saw the woodsman sitting

at his breakfast table, with a bowl of steaming food in front of him. He noticed that every time the man took a spoonful he would blow on it for a few seconds before eating it. The Martian asked the man's wife "Why is he doing that?"

'Why, he is cooling it, because it is very hot,' was the reply.

After finishing breakfast, the woodsman took his axe and went into the forest. The Martian decided to follow him, because he was interested in everything he did. He watched him swinging his axe as he cut up trees into logs for the fire.

After a while, the woodsman put down his axe and began blowing on his hands. "What is he doing now?" the Martian asked the woodsman's wife, who had just joined them with some hot food.

'Why, he is warming his hands because they are so cold', came the reply.

Immediately the Martian ran away, because anyone who can blow hot and cold air out of the same mouth must be very dangerous!"

What could I say? It's true. That is what financial people seem to do. They debit one thing and increase it, and then debit another and decrease it – no wonder managers flee from such things.

The golden rules of double entry

Now that I have explained the logic and origins of the double entry system, I feel I dare write down the rules that most financial people have to learn by heart, even if they do not understand why. They are:

1. Debit entries are written on the left hand side of the account, and credit entries are written on the right.
2. Debit the account that receives and credit the account that gives.
3. Debits increase the values of asset and expense accounts and decrease the value of liability and revenue accounts.
4. Credits decrease the value of asset and expense accounts and increase the value of liability and revenue accounts.
5. Every debit must have a corresponding credit (to ensure a zero balance).

I know that Andrew likes to see concepts graphically so here is a simplified diagram to illustrate them:

Figure 10.5 - Debits and credits Illustrated

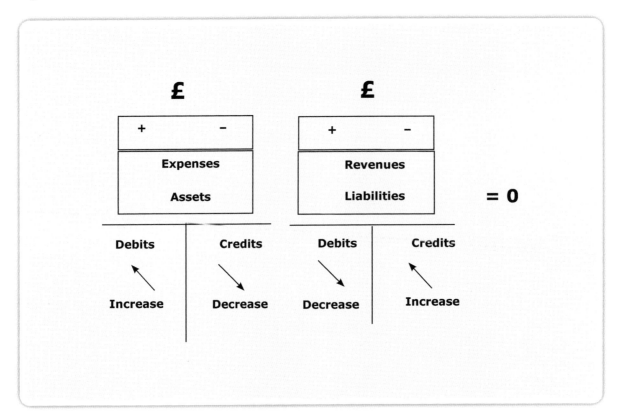

Here the liabilities and revenues are counterbalancing the assets and the expenses, so that the equation always equals zero, and because of the line separating the debits from the credits, these accounts are called 'T accounts.'

Andrew appreciated my diagram and insisted on taking a copy with him as they were leaving.

Double entry is a great system. Although Pacioli did not know it, his formulation of it was already in a form that could be transferred onto computers – as we demonstrated throughout this book. Packages, such as QuickBooks or Sage all have it incorporated within them.

Of one thing I am sure, when we do get to the stars, we will take the Pacioli method with us!

Summary

The Double entry System

An Italian monk, Luca Pacioli, described this framework in 1494. He was the first to explain how, by using debits and credits, the use of minus signs could be avoided.

He started with a simple equation based on the truism that

$$1 = 1$$

Pacioli rearranged his equation into the form

$$1 - 1 = 0$$

Since this was self-balancing, he could now ignore the equals sign (=) and the zero.

Next, he decided to use two columns under each main column heading to record the increases and decreases that were taking place. So we get:

Assets⁺ + Assets⁻ + Expenses⁺ + Expenses⁺ + Liabilities⁺ + Liabilities⁻ + Revenues⁺ + Revenues⁻ = 0

Because all the signs between the headings were positive they were superfluous and there was no need to attach signs to the numbers either, as these were implied by whether they were located in positive or negative columns. Balances were obtained by adding both columns and putting a balancing figure in the smaller of the two, itself being balanced by an equal entry in the opposite column under the ruled off totals.

Financial people are not the only ones who go to such lengths to avoid minuses; when using navigation tables to find their position, sailors only have to add numbers too. Come to think of it, mistakes made in navigation could mean the ship ending up on the rocks – and the same is true for companies if they mess up their finances as well!

Next he considered the terms **debit** and **credit**.

He realised that the verb **Debere** translates as obligation, accountability, or charge and **Credere** translates as trust, belief, and faith. Thus, when a company receives things for which it has to account, it has an obligation, so the amount is entered as a debit. The person who hands over these things to the company trusts it, has faith in it, so his account is credited.

Ledgers and financial records

The transaction spreadsheet provides a concise, global overview of how individual transactions change the financial structure of a business. In practical situations it would be cumbersome to use just one large spreadsheet, as there would be so many columns and entries to be made. Therefore, the spreadsheet is, in effect, cut up into individual pages that can be kept in books, called ledgers. Even commercially available computerised systems such as QuickBooks and Sage, for example, follow Pacioli's rules, and they all have the spreadsheet concept at their heart.

The five golden rules of double entry

No need to repeat them here. They are just a few pages back, if you need them.

I want to finish with a quotation from Pacioli's original treatise, since it is so like the subtitle of this book and the little poem I started with:

**"He who does business without knowing all about it,
sees his money go like flies."**

Glossary of Terms

Accounting Period

Usually the time between consecutive annual balance sheets, but it can be for shorter periods, such as a month, or even a week.

Accounting Policies

Where there is a possibility of choice between methods of calculating certain items, such as depreciation, a company sets out its chosen alternatives. Their choices will be guided by published accounting standards.

Accounting Standards

A series of rules and guidelines issued by a recognised accounting authority, such as the FRC – Financial Reporting Council – and the IFRC – International Financial Reporting Council

Accounts Payable

Suppliers to whom money is owed for goods or services that have been received, but for which they have not yet been paid, also called Creditors in the UK

Accounts Receivable

Customers who owe money for goods or services that have been supplied, but for which they have not yet paid, also called Debtors in the UK

Accruals

Expenses that are recognised when the goods received or services provided during a given period have been used up, but for which invoices have not been received by the end of the period; or when wages have been earned but have not yet been paid by the end of the period.

Accruals Convention

A convention under which the measurement of profit is based on the revenues achieved and the expenses incurred during a period, not on the cash actually received or payments made in that period.

Added Value

The difference between the price paid by a company for the goods and services bought from suppliers outside the company, and the price at which it sells the goods and services it provides for customers outside the company. It focuses attention on what is happening inside the company, and is made up of the following constituent elements:

Employee Costs + Capital Usage Costs (Depreciation) = Conversion Cost

Conversion cost + Net Profit (made up of tax, dividends and retained profit) = Net Added Value

Net Added Value + Capital Service Costs (Loan/ Overdraft Interest Etc.) = Gross Added Value

Administration Overheads	See General Overheads.
Amortisation	The process of writing off a financial asset over a period of time.
Assets	Economic resources that are expected to benefit future activities. A useful distinction can be made between operating assets and facilitating assets. Operating assets are intended to create more cash over their lifetimes than they cost. Cash itself is a facilitating asset – it does not create cash until it has been converted to an operating asset; a definition that includes an interest bearing deposit.
Balance Sheet	A statement of the financial structure of a business at a given date. It shows the composition of its assets and liabilities. It is a snapshot of the business, taken at a particular moment in time. There are alternative ways of presenting it.
Book Value	The historical cost of an asset. Not to be confused with current market value. See Net Book Value also
Break–even Analysis	An analysis of cost behaviour undertaken to assess the profit (or loss) likely to be achieved at various levels of business activity
Break–even Chart	A chart that shows the approximate profit or loss yielded at different levels of sales activity within a limited range.
Break–even Point	The level of activity at which there is neither a profit nor a loss, because the total revenue is exactly equal to the total costs of the business. This point is calculated by dividing the fixed costs by the contribution per unit of activity.
Burden	American term for manufacturing overhead costs.
Capital	This word is too general to use by itself. See Capital Employed, Operating Capital Employed, Equity, and Loan Capital.
Capital Employed	The funds used in a business to carry on its trading operations. It is made up of the owners' (or shareholders') equity plus both long–term and short–term loans and overdrafts. The definition used to be confined to equity and long–term loans, but it is now common practice for companies to include short–term funding in their financial strategies, for which the term Operating Capital Employed is a more precise definition. Many analysts still use the term Capital Employed for both definitions.

Capital Expenditure	Expenditure on assets who's anticipated working life extends beyond the year of purchase, usually for many future accounting periods.
Capital Growth	The extent by which a company's equity expands or shrinks as a result of the profit retained in the business during a given period of time. The difference between capital growth and operational growth is represented by the amount of dividends distributed to – or withdrawals made by – its owners.
Cash Discount	Discount allowed by suppliers for the prompt settlement of their accounts. Often known as a settlement discount, this is generally calculated as a percentage on the gross invoiced amount, and will not affect the unit price of goods covered by the invoice. Settlement discounts allowed and received are dealt with in separate accounts.
Cash Flow Forecast	A statement that analyses all cash receipts and payments over the periods during which the transactions are expected to take place. It enables any potential shortages or surpluses to be anticipated, and gives sufficient time for appropriate remedial action to be taken.
Cash Flow Statement	A statement that summarises all cash receipts and payments for a period. If prepared for internal use within a company it starts with amounts received from trading operations, from which payments made in respect of trading operations are deducted. Receipts and payments relating to investments and financial charges are then detailed separately. Published cash flow statements are presented in a more complex way.
Contribution	The difference between sales revenue and the variable cost of those sales. To break even a successful business must generate sufficient contribution to cover all its fixed costs. It is only after it has covered these costs that it starts to contribute towards a profit.
Cost	The sacrifice made to acquire goods or services. It may be a purchase price or it may be made up of manufacturing expenditures, if the goods or services are produced by the company itself. See also opportunity cost.
Cost of Goods Sold	The cost of the merchandise, or of the services rendered that can be directly associated with the sales revenue earned in the period.
Credit Entry	An entry made on the right–hand side of an account.
Credit Period	The time given to customers before they are expected to settle their bills.

Current Assets	Cash plus assets which are reasonably expected to be converted into cash, such as inventories and accounts receivable, or consumed within the business, within the next twelve months.
Current Liabilities	Liabilities that will be due for payment within the next twelve months.
Debit	An entry made on the left–hand side of an account.
Depletion	The using up of natural land resources, as in mines and quarries, etc. This is based on a technical assessment of the number of resource units likely to be yielded – i.e., tonnes or cubic metres, etc. – rather than on the number of years likely to be spent on the extraction process.
Depreciation	The charge made against the trading profits of a period to reflect the cost to the company of using up its Noncurrent Assets during that period. It is not a cash transaction. The most common method of calculating this cost is the straight line method, under which the estimated end–of–life value is deducted from the acquisition cost to arrive at a net cost. This net cost is then spread evenly over the number of years of its anticipated useful life. See also the reducing balance method, and the sum of year's digits method.
Discounts	See trade discount and cash discount.
Dividend	An amount suggested by the directors to be paid to the shareholders out of the profits available in the company. It has to be voted upon by the shareholders at the annual general meeting.
Dividend cover Earnings before	Profit after tax divided by the dividend.
Interest and tax	The profits earned from the operations of the company before including any interest, whether received or paid, and before charging tax.
Equity	The owner(s) risk–carrying capital stake in a business, made up of their original capital investment (the nominal amount of their shares), plus the accumulated profits, and reserves.
Equity Balance Sheet	A presentation of the balance sheet in which long–term liabilities are deducted from the book value of the company's net assets, to arrive at a figure that is equal to the shareholders funds. It thus focuses primarily on the shareholders' view of the company. It is the most frequently used of the two official formats for published accounts allowed under the Companies Acts.

Expenditure	An expenditure takes place the moment you pay for goods or services that you are buying – whether or not this is before or after the period during which they are actually used up, or expensed.
Expense	The amount of a resource (or asset) that is used up, that is, expensed, during the period under review. It is calculated in terms of its original cost to the business. For long term assets see depreciation.
Financial Charges	Expenses related to the financing of business operations, such as loan interest, bank charges, etc. These need to be separated from purely operational expenses in the income statement.
Financial Liabilities	Loans and bank overdrafts made to a company.
Fixed Assets	Tangible assets that a company acquires to provide goods or services during and beyond the current financial period, rather than for resale in the normal course of trading.
Fixed Costs	Costs that are unaffected by activity within certain limits.
General Overheads	Expenses incurred in the centralised marketing, research, and administration areas of a business.
Gross Balance sheet	A presentation of the balance sheet in which the total of a company's assets is balanced against the total of its liabilities. This presentation is rarely used in published accounts nowadays.
Gross Margin	Gross profit divided by sales revenue, expressed as a percentage.
Gross Profit	The excess of sales revenue over the cost of goods sold, before deducting expenses incurred in selling, distribution or administration costs, or financial and taxation charges, etc.
Growth	See operational growth and capital growth.
Income	Also known as Profit. The measurement of growth or shrinkage arising out of the activities of a business during any given period. It is the difference between the revenues for that period and all the expenses and charges for that period.
Income Statement	A statement that gives a detailed summary of the revenues and expenses of a trading period. Also called Profit and Loss account; the company's history book.
Input Tax	The tax paid by a customer on the goods or services purchased from its registered suppliers. See also value added tax.

Inventory	Any goods held for conversion into cash in the normal course of trading, e.g., raw materials, work–in–progress, finished goods, goods in transit, or on sale or return; sometimes called stock in the UK.
Investment	An outlay of cash or its equivalent, in the anticipation of obtaining a greater amount at sometime in the future. It is speculative by nature.
Liability	A financial obligation to pay, or repay money that is owed to someone else.
Limited Company	A company whose shareholders only stand to lose their share capital, hence their liability is limited. They are not liable for the company's debts personally.
Liquid Assets	Current assets that can be almost immediately converted back into cash – e.g., cash itself, accounts receivable balances, short– term investments, etc., but not inventories in most cases.
Loan	Money owed for a specified period of time, with a specified interest rate and repayment schedule.
Long–term Debt	Long–term external loans and operating liabilities.
Long–term Liabilities	Amounts that are not due for repayment during the next twelve months.
Long–term Plans	Financial projections, covering several periods ahead, often for five to ten years.
Loss	The excess of expenses over revenue.
Managed Cost	One that is dependent on management decisions – such as the advertising expenses in the Andycabs example. Once the budget has been set, it is regarded as a fixed cost.
Matching Principle	See accruals convention.
Medium–term plan	Summarised annual plans, generally covering two to five years ahead. They will not be in too much detail, but should be sufficiently researched to make them readily convertible into detailed, rolling short–term plans.
Money	A medium that can be exchanged for goods and services. It is also useful for measuring and comparing items.
Net assets	The amount of a company's total assets, less its short–term (operating and financial) liabilities or, alternatively, the sum of its Noncurrent Assets plus its Working Capital. It is equivalent to the total of the company's Equity and long–term external debt. If the equity balance sheet method id used then Net Assets are equal to Equity. The Operating Capital employed format gives a better figure fir Net Assets. Check the definitions that are being used.

Net Assets Balance Sheet	A presentation of the balance sheet in which a company's Net Assets is balanced against its long-term liabilities, including equity
Net Current Assets	See Working Capital.
Non-operational Income	Income of a non-operational nature, such as investment income or interest receivable. This income has to be shown separately in the income statement.
Operating Capital Employed	Shareholders' funds plus noncurrent liabilities plus short term loans. It equals Operating Net Assets
Operating Expenses	Expenses connected with the operational activities of a company, such as supplies and services used, employee costs, etc. See also overhead costs.
Operating Liabilities	Liabilities connected with the operational activities of a company. They will be classified as either short-term or long-term, depending on whether they are due for settlement within the next twelve months.
Operating Net Assets	The amount of a company's total assets, less its current operating liabilities. It is equivalent to Operating Capital Employed.
Operating Profit	The profit made out of the purely operational activities of a business – before taking into account non-operational income and expenses, loan interest, taxation or shareholders' dividends. Also known as trading profit.
Operational Growth/Shrinkage	The extent by which a business expands or shrinks as a result of its operational activities during a given period of time. It is measured by its profit after tax.
Opportunity Cost	The value of a benefit sacrificed in favour of an alternative course of action.
Output Tax	The tax levied by a registered supplier on the goods or services sold to its customers. See value added tax.
Overdraft	Funds provided by a bank on a day-to-day basis and repayable on demand. They may be secured by a charge on some of the company's assets.
Prepayments	Payments made in one period in respect of items that will be expensed against the profits of future periods.
Profit after Tax	The net profit left to the owners or shareholders of a business, after the deduction of operational, financial and taxation charges.
Profit before Tax	The net profit due to the owners or shareholders of a business, before the deduction of tax, but after the deduction of loan interest charges.

Profit before Interest and tax–BIT)	The profit made by a business, before taking into account non– operational income and expenses, such as interest received and paid, and before the deduction of taxation or shareholders dividends.
Profit Graph	American term for break–even chart. Profit Reserves. The accumulated profit retained in a company, rather than being distributed as dividends. They can be used for any purpose, unlike other reserves, which can only be used for the purpose for which they were specifically created.
Provision	An amount charged against profit to reduce the recorded value of an asset in the period that a potential loss is recognised, or to cover an expected liability, when the exact amount or timing of the liability is uncertain. Known in the USA as reserves.
Quick Ratio	See acid test ratio. Reducing Balance Method of calculating depreciation in which the amount of the original cost of an asset charged to each period is based on a constant percentage of its progressively reducing balance.
Reserves	Part of a company's Equity capital, arising out of accumulated undistributed profits, or the effects of company policy. Retained Profits Often known as revenue reserves. They are available for distribution as dividends, whereas capital reserves are not. Capital reserves are reserves created as a result of company policy, such as the revaluation of Noncurrent Assets, or the issue of shares at a premium price. These must be specifically identified under such headings as revaluation reserve, or share premium reserve, etc. the term reserves is also used in America for what we call provisions in the UK. See also profit reserves, revenue reserves, revaluation reserve, and share premium reserve.
Revenue	The income of a business, achieved via the proceeds of sales, or investment income, etc.
Revenue Expenditure	Money spent on items that are to be expensed, or charged in full against the revenues of the current year.
Revenue Reserve	See profit reserve.
Saving	Setting funds aside for future use.
Settlement discount	See cash discount.
Share	A fixed unit of capital contributed by a member of a company – the shareholder. It entitles the investor to a share in the ownership of the company, and to share in its profits.

Share Capital	The nominal value of the issued share capital. It is not related in any way to the market values of those shares, which is decided by buyers and sellers on the open market.
Share Price.	The market value of a share, decided by buyers and sellers.
Short-term Plan	A detailed plan covering a short period, usually of up to the next twelve months. All revenues and expenses should be forecast and controlled in as much detail as practicable, so that the progress of strategies can be monitored, adjusted or corrected if necessary.
Stepped Costs	Costs that are affected by significant incremental amounts at certain levels of activity. Most costs only behave in a truly fixed or variable way within certain limits.
Stock	Raw materials, work-in-progress, finished goods, goods in transit, or on sale or return. The American term for this is Inventory. They use the term 'stock' to refer to shares issued on a Stock Exchange.

Straight Line Method of Calculating

Depreciation	This is the simplest, and most commonly used method of calculating depreciation, under which the net cost of the asset is first established by deducting its estimated end-of-life disposal value from its acquisition cost. This net cost is then spread evenly over the anticipated number of years' useful working life.
	Sum of Years Digits Method of calculating depreciation in which the number of years of an asset's anticipated life is listed in descending order and totaled. The amount of depreciation charged to each year is in proportion to that years digit related to the total. For instance, over a five-year period, the digits would be 5, 4, 3, 2 and 1, and the sum of these digits would be (5 + 4 + 3 + 2 + 1 =) 15. 5/15ths of the cost would thus be charged to the first year, 4/15ths to the second, and so on.
Suspense	A temporary home for entries until sufficient information is available for them to be recorded correctly.
T-Account	An account listing where the entries are recorded under the twin column system. It is so-called because of the rulings on the page that underline the title, and that divide the left-hand (debit) entries from the right-hand (credit) entries.
Trade Discount	Discount allowed by suppliers from their list prices for goods purchased in bulk quantities, or for wholesale distribution to the trade.

Transaction Equation	An equation that records both the receiving and the giving sides of a financial transaction.
Trial Balance	A list of all the balances in a company's accounts.
Value Added Tax	The difference between the output tax levied by a business on the goods or services sold to its customers, and the input tax paid on the goods and services purchased from its suppliers. Businesses whose annual revenue exceeds a certain amount have to register for VAT, and, once registered, they act as a collecting agency for the government – passing on the net amount due to H.M. Customs and Excise. The net amount passed on is equivalent to a tax on the cost of converting the goods and services purchased into the goods or services sold. This conversion process represents the value added to the goods and services purchased, and will be made up of employee costs and capital usage costs like depreciation.
Variable Costs	Costs that vary with changes in the level of activity. Also known as marginal costs, or, in America, as direct costs. The American definition should not be confused with the UK definition of direct cost, which can include an element of directly attributable fixed costs.
What if? Analysis	A form of sensitivity analysis performed on the financial model of a business situation.
Working Capital	The difference between a company's Current Assets and its Current Liabilities. It can also be defined as the net amount of Current Assets that need to be funded out of the company's Long– Term Capital.
Written–down Value	See book value.

Printed in Great Britain
by Amazon